History Comes Alive Teaching Unit

PIONEERS

by
Susan Moger

SCHOLASTIC
PROFESSIONAL BOOKS

NEW YORK · TORONTO · LONDON · AUCKLAND · SYDNEY
MEXICO CITY · NEW DELHI · HONG KONG

DEDICATION

This book is dedicated to my father, Roy W. Moger,
who taught me that history is a story to be relished in the telling and
to my grandmother, Edna I. Moger, who was born in a blizzard
in 1882 in Carson City, Nevada,
and never lost touch with her western roots.

ACKNOWLEDGMENTS

In writing this book I received help and advice from many people: Larry and Tigi Armour gave me insights into technology, quilting, and the delights of recreating history; Ted Armour provided unflagging interest and encouragement; and Rachel Moger-Reischer, my niece, inspired me to make it fun.

I am indebted to Virginia Dooley for guiding the book to its destination and to the following people for making it beautiful: Josué Castilleja, Solutions by Design, and Jenny Williams.

CREDITS

Cover Photos

Nebraska State Historical Society; Brigham Young University; and Denver Public Library, Western History Department

Interior Photos

Pages: 5: North Wind Pictures; 7: Colorado Department of Public Relations; 15: Dept. of the Interior; 19: Nebraska State Historical Society; 31: Denver Public Library, Western History Department; 51: Brigham Young University; 61: Nebraska State Historical Society; 64: Denver Public Library, Western History Department; 68: Courtesy of Mott Media, Fenton, MI 48430.

Excerpts

Westward Bound, 1842 by Samuel Murray Stover, Library Collection, University of Oklahoma; *Dakota in the Morning* by William Harlowe Briggs © William Harlowe Briggs, Farrar & Rinehart, 1942; *The Long Winter* by Laura Ingalls Wilder © Laura Ingalls Wilder, HarperCollins, 1971; *North Star Country* by Meridel Le Sueur © Meridel Le Sueur (American Folkways series) Duell, Sloan & Pearce, New York 1945. *Pioneer Women* by Joanna Stratton © Joanna Stratton, Simon & Schuster, 1981; *Women's Diaries of the Westward Journey* by Lillian Schlissel © Schocken Books, 1992.

Cover design by Josué Castilleja
Interior design by Solutions by Design, Inc.
Interior illustrations by Jenny Williams

ISBN: 0-439-13845-0

Table of Contents

PART 4: SETTLING THE GREAT PLAINS—1860s–1880s

EPILOGUE: NATIVE AMERICANS—END OF AN ERA

INTRODUCTION

I n Katherine Lee Bates' 1893 song, "America the Beautiful," the words "from sea to shining sea" celebrate a dream come true: the nation that had started as thirteen states clinging to the Atlantic shore now spanned an entire continent. The process had taken less than 100 years.

The official, government-sanctioned opening of the Far West began with the Louisiana Purchase in 1803 and the subsequent explorations of the Corps of Discovery, headed by Lewis and Clark. By the last decade of the nineteenth century the West had become part of the United States. People moving west had changed the shape of the United States. In the process they had changed irrevocably the world of the continent's original inhabitants, Native Americans.

Heading west has always been the American dream. The West in the national mythology is a landscape of freedom. Yet the pioneers who traveled west took their problems, fears, concerns, and biases along with them. We know that because they tell us. On the Oregon Trail, in the California gold fields, on the Great Plains, they wrote journals, diaries, and letters back home. These firsthand accounts are powerful documents. Reading them brings history to life. We see not just a stream of faceless, nameless settlers but individuals, like Samuel Murray Stover who wrote about his journey to the California gold fields in 1849. His account touches on his animals, terrifying storms, and the lives and deaths of his companions in the wagon train. His diary, like the diaries of other pioneers, reveals the courage and persistence of people engaged in an immense undertaking—the move west.

In this book, your students will learn about the pioneers through firsthand accounts and hands-on activities focusing on two great waves of western settlement: the movement of people to Oregon and California in the 1840s and 1850s and onto the Great Plains in the 1860s–1880s. They will explore the world of Native Americans on the Great Plains before and after the waves of settlers and learn how the great buffalo herds, lifeblood of the Plains Indians, were decimated.

The story of western settlement is a crazy quilt of varied attitudes and experiences. In this book students will learn about the great prizes that were won in the West and the high prices that were paid in blood and tears. They will also meet individuals who played a role in western settlement—from the famous, such as Sitting Bull, to the anonymous voices quoted by the folklorist Meridel LeSeuer. It is these individual stories that make the big story of the westward movement so compelling. We as a nation have never tired of hearing it.

TIME LINE

KEY DATES IN WESTERN SETTLEMENT

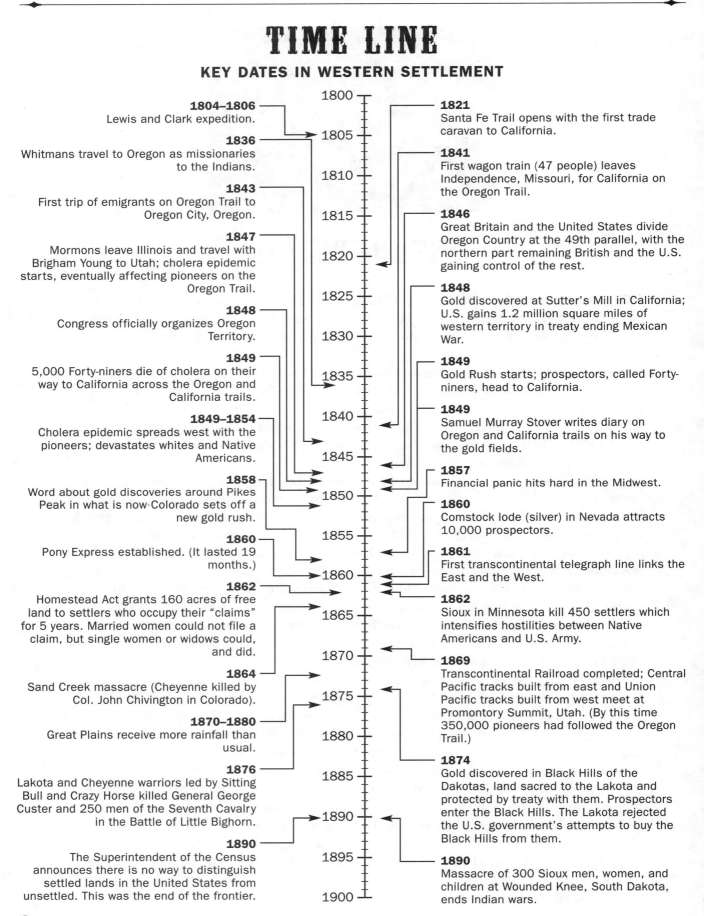

1804–1806
Lewis and Clark expedition.

1836
Whitmans travel to Oregon as missionaries to the Indians.

1843
First trip of emigrants on Oregon Trail to Oregon City, Oregon.

1847
Mormons leave Illinois and travel with Brigham Young to Utah; cholera epidemic starts, eventually affecting pioneers on the Oregon Trail.

1848
Congress officially organizes Oregon Territory.

1849
5,000 Forty-niners die of cholera on their way to California across the Oregon and California trails.

1849–1854
Cholera epidemic spreads west with the pioneers; devastates whites and Native Americans.

1858
Word about gold discoveries around Pikes Peak in what is now Colorado sets off a new gold rush.

1860
Pony Express established. (It lasted 19 months.)

1862
Homestead Act grants 160 acres of free land to settlers who occupy their "claims" for 5 years. Married women could not file a claim, but single women or widows could, and did.

1864
Sand Creek massacre (Cheyenne killed by Col. John Chivington in Colorado).

1870–1880
Great Plains receive more rainfall than usual.

1876
Lakota and Cheyenne warriors led by Sitting Bull and Crazy Horse killed General George Custer and 250 men of the Seventh Cavalry in the Battle of Little Bighorn.

1890
The Superintendent of the Census announces there is no way to distinguish settled lands in the United States from unsettled. This was the end of the frontier.

1800
1805
1810
1815
1820
1825
1830
1835
1840
1845
1850
1855
1860
1865
1870
1875
1880
1885
1890
1895
1900

1821
Santa Fe Trail opens with the first trade caravan to California.

1841
First wagon train (47 people) leaves Independence, Missouri, for California on the Oregon Trail.

1846
Great Britain and the United States divide Oregon Country at the 49th parallel, with the northern part remaining British and the U.S. gaining control of the rest.

1848
Gold discovered at Sutter's Mill in California; U.S. gains 1.2 million square miles of western territory in treaty ending Mexican War.

1849
Gold Rush starts; prospectors, called Forty-niners, head to California.

1849
Samuel Murray Stover writes diary on Oregon and California trails on his way to the gold fields.

1857
Financial panic hits hard in the Midwest.

1860
Comstock lode (silver) in Nevada attracts 10,000 prospectors.

1861
First transcontinental telegraph line links the East and the West.

1862
Sioux in Minnesota kill 450 settlers which intensifies hostilities between Native Americans and U.S. Army.

1869
Transcontinental Railroad completed; Central Pacific tracks built from east and Union Pacific tracks built from west meet at Promontory Summit, Utah. (By this time 350,000 pioneers had followed the Oregon Trail.)

1874
Gold discovered in Black Hills of the Dakotas, land sacred to the Lakota and protected by treaty with them. Prospectors enter the Black Hills. The Lakota rejected the U.S. government's attempts to buy the Black Hills from them.

1890
Massacre of 300 Sioux men, women, and children at Wounded Knee, South Dakota, ends Indian wars.

6

Part 1

THE WEST

INTRODUCTION

What and where is "the West" to which so many people traveled during the nineteenth century? Depending on where they started from, "west" was anything beyond the horizon where the sun set. For some people "the West" meant Oregon or California, the farthest west one could travel before reaching the Pacific Ocean. For others it meant what we now call Nebraska, Kansas, South Dakota, Montana, Colorado, or Texas.

Whatever the geographic destination, long before there were any western states in the United States, "West" was a state of mind, an attitude about what a person could become. The decision to travel west was, for many white settlers, "a moral decision" to transform wilderness into settled, "civilized" land.

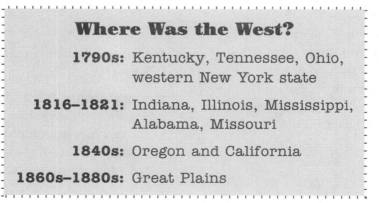

Where Was the West?

1790s: Kentucky, Tennessee, Ohio, western New York state

1816–1821: Indiana, Illinois, Mississippi, Alabama, Missouri

1840s: Oregon and California

1860s–1880s: Great Plains

ACTIVITIES

The Shape of the Land

Students create models of the physical features of the western United States in order to understand better the obstacles that the pioneers had to overcome.

MATERIALS

Outline map and topographic map of the United States

Living Relief Map

Nylon cord, masking tape, or chalk to outline the shape of the United States, large enough for 30 students to stand inside; yellow police tape or long rope to represent the Continental Divide

Papier-Mâché Map (for each pair of students)

Sheet of cardboard; paper towels torn into small pieces; paints, brushes, thin markers, pens, and paper (for making labels); white glue (8 tablespoons); 1 small bowl; water (8 tablespoons)

BACKGROUND

The geography of the western United States influenced the history of the West and of the country. A hunger for land, born of frustration with the declining opportunities in the East, made many people look west. But geographic features, such as mountains, rivers, and deserts, were daunting obstacles facing pioneers. The Rocky Mountains, the largest mountain range in North America, is a chain of mountains 3,000 miles long. Pioneers crossing the Rockies passed over the Continental Divide, an imaginary line that follows the highest ridge of the mountains. On the east side of the Continental Divide, rivers flow toward the Mississippi River, while rivers on the west side flow toward the Pacific Ocean.

WHAT TO DO

⊗ To help students visualize the geographic features pioneers met traveling west on the Oregon Trail, read to the class the following description:

> From the main jump-off point at Independence, Missouri, the Oregon Trail angled west across the Kansas grasslands, and north into Nebraska. From there it continued west by a bit north along the broad, silt-clogged Platte River, rising...through the Nebraska prairies and onto the high, desolate [Great] Plains.
>
> Past Fort Laramie, in what would one day become the state of Wyoming, the trail climbed gradually through an undulating landscape...toward the snow-capped ranges of the Rocky Mountains. It crossed the Continental Divide at...South Pass...[a] broad flat corridor through the Rockies....
>
> After crossing South Pass, the trail entered the arid eastern regions of the Oregon country, an area too harsh...to invite settlement....[T]he trail descend[ed] the slope of the continent along the torturous curve of the Snake River that cut through a succession of difficult mountain ranges before joining the Columbia [River]....
>
> —Huston Horn, *The Old West: The Pioneers,* Time-Life Books, 1974.

⊗ Define *silt, Continental Divide, undulating,* and *arid.*

⊗ Ask students: What kind of obstacle does a *mountain* present to people traveling on foot or in a wagon pulled by oxen? What about a *plain?* A *desert?* A *river?* How could travelers overcome these obstacles?

⊗ Trace the journey described in the quotation on a large topographic map of the United

States. Identify the Mississippi River, the Great Plains, the Rocky Mountains, the Great Basin, the Sierra Nevada, the Cascade Range.

✵ Introduce the word "elevation," a measurement of the distance between sea level and a specific place on the surface of the earth.

✵ Explain to students that to understand the shape of the land west of the Mississippi, they will create relief maps.

Make a "Living" Relief Map

On a playground or in the school gymnasium, use nylon rope or masking tape to outline the shape of the United States. Make it large enough for 30 students to stand inside with room to move around.

Mountains

Students will stand in north-south lines to represent the following mountain ranges (from east to west): Appalachian and Adirondack Mountains; Rocky Mountains; Sierra Nevada and Cascade Range; Coast Range. (Use the topographic map to establish the relative position of the ranges within the borders of the United States.)

Continental Divide

Ask three of four students to hold a yellow police tape or long rope to indicate the Continental Divide.

Coastal Plain, Central Lowlands, Great Plains, and Great Basin

Students kneel or squat to show these topographic features. To identify which they represent, they can make signs to hold.

Make Papier-Mâché Maps

✵ Pass out a sheet of cardboard and an outline map of the United States to pairs of students. Ask students to cut out the shape of the continental United States and glue it on the piece of cardboard. Using a large classroom map of the United States as a reference, they can draw in features such as the Mississippi River and the Great Lakes.

✵ Have students work in groups of four. Give each group supplies for making papier-mâché (see page 8). Tell students to mix the bits of paper with the glue and water until the mixture is wet and looks like lumpy mashed potatoes. Add more glue or water as needed. Hang a topographical map of the United States on the board.

✵ Have students spread the mixture on their maps, starting at the western coast and spreading the mixture inland to the Mississippi. They should completely cover the map west of the Mississippi. Once the mixture covers the western part of the map, they should refer to the topographic map and pinch up the mountains (adding more of the mixture as needed) and flatten the Great Basin and the Great Plains. Allow maps to dry before painting them.

✵ Have students paint their maps, using the topographical map in your classroom as a guide. After students have painted the terrain, have them use a blue pen to draw the rivers, such as the Columbia, the Platte, the Missouri, and the Green. They can then use different colored pens to mark the Oregon and California trails. Finally, students can make small identifying labels and glue them on their maps.

Footprints of Time

To forge a link between students and local Native Americans, students identify roads that were once Indian trails in their town or state.

MATERIALS

Local histories of town, county, or state; street address or e-mail address of local, county, or state historians; copies of street maps of town or county; road maps of state

BACKGROUND

Many of the trails used in the great westward migrations of pioneers in the 1840s–1880s were originally Indian trails. (The "wilderness" was not wild from an Indian's perspective.) In many parts of the country today streets, roads, and highways follow the paths made by Indians centuries ago. Some historians believe that many of the trails in the western United States followed the north-south migratory paths of the buffalo herds and the Indians who hunted them.

WHAT TO DO

⊗ To make the point that there was no "wilderness" to the Indians of North America, read students the following quote from the historian Alvin Josephy, Jr.

> [Before the arrival of Europeans] [h]undreds of unique Indian nations blanketed the entire continent....Some [were] nomadic, most permanently settled in communities that ranged in size up to cities as large and sophisticated as any in the world at that time. Every part of the land and all of the natural world...was sacred to one Indian nation or another.
>
> —Alvin Josephy, Jr., *500 Nations, An Illustrated History of North American Indians*, Alfred A. Knopf, 1994.

⊗ Ask a group of students to research the early history of your town, county, or state to identify Native Americans who once lived there and determine which Indian trails became roads that are still in use today.

⊗ On a copy of a current map, mark the roads that coincide with Indian trails.

EXTEND THE LESSON

⊗ Ask a group of students to find out more about local Native Americans, then and now, and report to the class. Invite a local historian or tribal representative to visit your class.

People of the Great Plains

Students learn that Native American tribes inhabited the land through which pioneers passed on their way to Oregon in the 1840s and where they settled in the 1860s–1880s. They identify the people met by pioneers along the Oregon Trail—Apache and Comanche on the southern Plains; the Arapaho, Kiowa, and Pawnee on the central Plains; Cheyenne, Lakota (Sioux), Blackfoot, Shoshone, and Crow on the northern Plains.

MATERIALS

Tribes of the West and Sign Language reproducibles (pages 13–14)

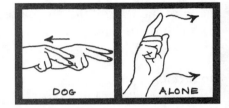

BACKGROUND

Moving west, pioneers in the 1840s–1880s first passed through and then settled on land that had been used by Native Americans for centuries. The first pioneers to move west on the Oregon Trail found Native Americans to be helpful not hostile.

WHAT TO DO

⊗ Explain that some Plains Indians, like the Dakota (called Sioux by their enemies) were relative newcomers to the Great Plains who had moved west as the East was settled. The Dakota in turn pushed out other tribes as they moved in.

⊗ Distribute the Sign Language reproducible and discuss the name of each tribe and its implications. Invite students to practice signing messages.

⊗ Provide students with copies of the map on page 13. Assign small groups of students different tribes to investigate and report on. They should include the following information in their reports: treatment of children, attitudes toward white settlers, traditional hunting grounds, religion, war practices.

Buffalo Nation

Students learn about the importance of the buffalo in the lives of the Plains Indians. They fold paper or cloth to make a small model of a parfleche, or carry-all, used by Plains Indians.

MATERIALS

The Buffalo (page 15), Parfleche Pattern (page 16), and Circular: to the Oregon Emigrants (page 17) reproducibles; canvas or heavy paper; hole punch; string; paints or markers

BACKGROUND

The pioneers who moved west (about 350,000 between 1843 and 1869) disrupted the migration of the buffalo herds, which numbered in the millions of animals. Wagons rolling across the Great Plains were the first step in the extinction of the buffalo and with them the Native American societies that depended on them.

A parfleche was rawhide pouch, usually about 13 inches x 26 inches in size, tied with rawhide strips. Parfleches were used by Plains Indians for storing dried meat or clothing.

WHAT TO DO

⊛ Present students with the following information:

In the 18th century, 75 million buffalo roamed the Great Plains; the Native American tribes that hunted the buffalo took them for granted, assuming that, like the ground beneath their feet, the buffalo would always be there. By 1874, due to overhunting, settlement, and the railroads, the great herds had been almost completely wiped out and with them the Indians who depended on them.

⊛ To establish the importance of the buffalo in the lives of the Plains Indians, distribute copies of The Buffalo reproducible. Read the selections with students and discuss them. Identify the point of view or bias of each writer (if possible).

⊛ Then identify the ways in which Indians used parts of the buffalo. Make a chart on the chalkboard, or have students make individual charts with these headings: "Food," "Clothing," "Weapons," "Transportation," "Shelter," "Tools and Objects." Use information from The Buffalo reproducible and other sources to complete the chart.

Make a Parfleche

⊛ Ask students what they would use to carry their lunch to school or on a picnic. List items on the chalkboard. They might include: lunch box or basket, paper bag, plastic bag, backpack, knapsack, purse, beach bag.

⊛ Then read students the following description of a parfleche:

> Great quantities of dried buffalo meat were stored in large folded rawhide cases, rather like envelopes, called parfleches. Bulging parfleches made a family feel secure against hunger. If there came a time when there was nothing left to eat, the parfleches empty, then everyone went hungry."
>
> —Paul Goble, *The Return of the Buffaloes*, (National Geographic Society, 1996).

⊛ Distribute the Parfleche Pattern, reproducible and explain to students that they are going to make a mini-parfleche out of cloth or paper.

⊛ Invite students to make the mini-parfleche and decorate it, following the instructions on the reproducible.

⊛ Display the parfleches in the classroom or have students write a note to parents to take home inside their parfleche. The note could describe what they are learning in class and contain directions for making a full-size parfleche at home.

⊛ Distribute the Circular reproducible and have students restate the message in their own words.

A simplified restatement of the Circular might be:

The Indians you meet on this trail are friendly. Please treat them with kindness. Travel in large groups to prevent theft. Indians sometimes steal from pioneers traveling in small groups. This is often because an earlier group broke a promise or cheated them. This shows how important it is to keep your word with them.

✪ Use the Circular to introduce a discussion of the ways pioneers and Native Americans interacted. Ask students the following questions:

- ⊙ Who posted the sign? (*the Governor of Oregon Territory, Superintendent of Indian Affairs*)

- ⊙ If you are a pioneer reading this sign, what does it tell you about the land you are passing through on your way to Oregon? (*It belongs to Indians.*)

- ⊙ Why have some pioneers been robbed of their belongings? (*Because earlier pioneers cheated the Indians.*)

- ⊙ Why do you think this Circular was posted along the trail? (*To influence the way pioneers dealt with Indians; to encourage them to travel in large groups; to let them know that Oregon had a "Superintendent of Indian Affairs."*)

- ⊙ In what way does the Circular show a lack of understanding of the Indians mentioned? (*It does not mention the name of specific tribes or nations.*)

EXTEND THE LESSON

Discuss other ways to convey this information to travelers rather than by posting it on a tree beside the trail.

TRIBES OF THE WEST

Pioneers traveling to the West might encounter many different Native American groups.

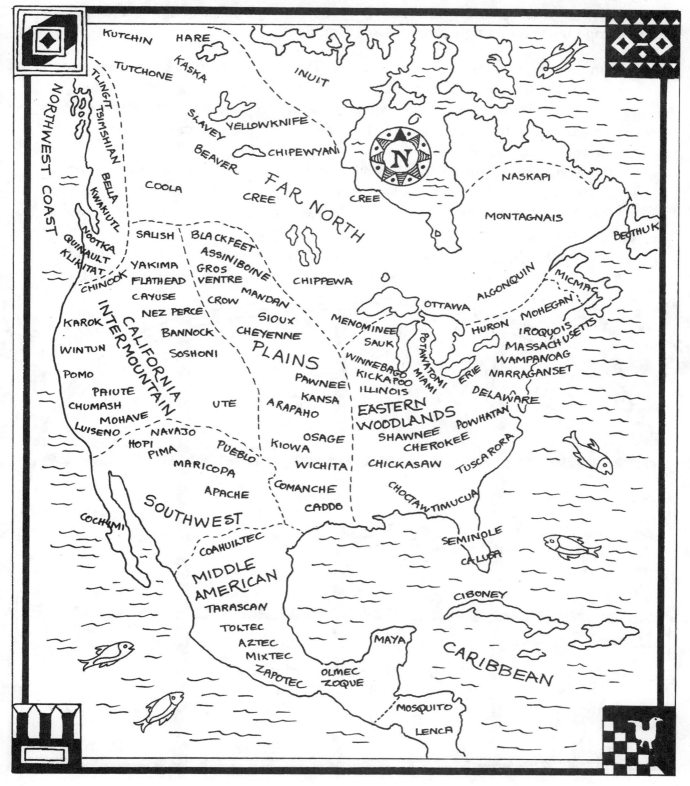

SIGN LANGUAGE

Sign language evolved out of necessity. The Plains Indian tribes spoke many different languages; sign language allowed them all to communicate. Captain Marcy describes sign language as "exceedingly graceful and significant."

[On meeting Indians who are strangers to you] they may be asked if they are friends by raising both hands grasped in the manner of shaking hands, or by locking the two forefingers firmly when the hands are held up. If friendly they will respond with the same signal....The pantomimic [sign] vocabulary is understood by all the Prairie Indians....

The Comanche is represented by making with the hand a waving motion in imitation of the crawling of a snake.

The Cheyenne or "Cut-arm," by drawing the hand across the arm, to imitate cutting it with a knife....

The Sioux [Dakota], or "Cut-throats," by drawing the hand across the throat.

—Randolph B. Marcy, Captain, U.S. Army, *The Prairie Traveler* [1859].

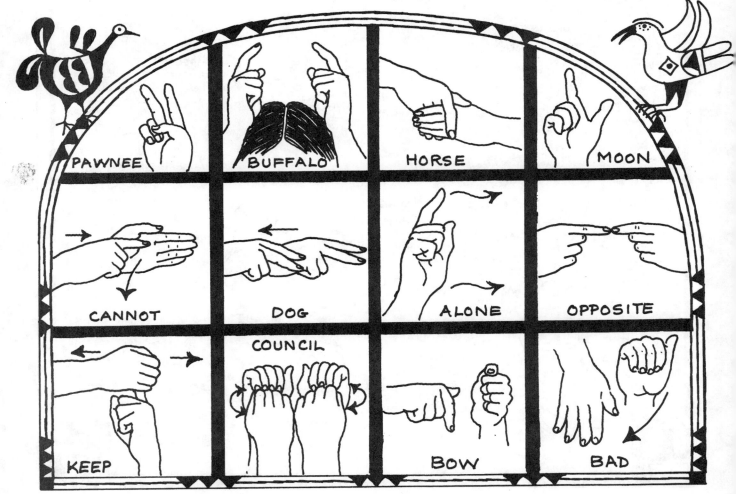

Name_____ Date_____

THE BUFFALO

Read the facts and excerpts below to learn more about the buffalo and its importance to Native Americans.

Everything the Kiowas had came from the buffalo. . .. Their tipis were made of buffalo hides, so were their clothes and moccasins. They ate buffalo meat. Their containers were made of hide, or of bladders or stomachs. . .. The buffalo were the life of the Kiowas.

   —Old Lady Horse, Kiowa

Prepare for me a pasture for the buffalo bull, his wife and young, at some distance so that by means of them I and my people may keep alive. Among them I shall survive.

   —Dakota Song

The largest and most useful animal that roams over the prairies is the buffalo. It provides food, clothing, and shelter to thousands of natives whose means of livelihood depend almost exclusively upon this gigantic monarch of the prairies. . .

  The buffalo has immense powers of endurance, and will run for many miles without any apparent effort or diminution in speed. The first buffalo I ever saw I followed about ten miles, and when I left him he seemed to run faster than when the chase commenced.

   —Randolph B. Marcy, Captain, U.S. Army, *The Prairie Traveler [1859]*.

Buffalo Facts

⊙ Until the mid-nineteenth century, there were tens of millions of buffalo on the Great Plains. As western travelers disrupted their grazing lands and built new trails and railroads across the Great Plains, the numbers fell.

⊙ A bull buffalo might weigh a ton and reach a height of six feet at the hump.

⊙ Buffalo usually traveled in small groups of five to 50 and sometimes massed in huge herds of several hundred thousand.

⊙ Buffalo had poor eyesight and slow wits, but their size and fierce response to attack made up for these shortcomings.

⊙ Between 1872 and 1874 at least 4 million buffalo were killed for their hides. The great herds were reduced to 20 buffalo by 1897.

PARFLECHE PATTERN

Follow the steps below to make your own parfleche.

1. Cut out the pattern along the solid lines.

2. Fold the long sides on the dotted lines so the ends meet in the middle.

3. Fold the two ends in to meet in the middle.

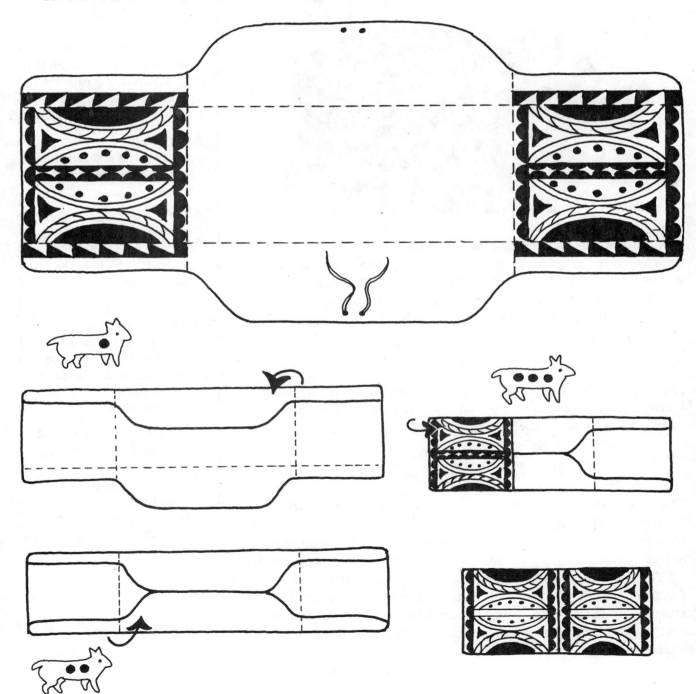

16

CIRCULAR

TO THE OREGON EMIGRANTS

Imagine seeing this weather-beaten notice posted along the Oregon Trail. You can read; your traveling companions cannot. How would you explain what it said?

Gentlemen:

[A]s Superintendent of Indian affairs, by an Act passed by the Legislature of Oregon, [I am charged with instructing]... Emigrants to this Territory...[how] "to maintain and promote peace and friendship between them and the Indian tribes through which they may pass." [A]llow me to say in the first place, that the Indians on the old road to this country [the Oregon Trail] are friendly to the whites. They should be treated with kindness on all occasions. ...Notwithstanding Indians are friendly, it is best to keep in good sized companies [large groups] while passing through their country. Small parties of two or three are sometimes stripped of their property while on their way to this Territory, perhaps because a preceding party promised to pay the Indians for something had of them, and failed to fulfill their promise. This will show you the necessity of keeping your word with them in all cases. ...

Dated at Oregon City, this 22d of April, 1847.

GEO. ABERNETHY,
Governor of Oregon Territory and
Superintendent of Indian Affairs

WHO WENT WEST? WHY DID THEY GO?

INTRODUCTION

From the time the first settlers arrived on the east coast of what became the United States, they began the process of migration—pushing farther and farther west. Throughout the eighteenth and nineteenth centuries, men and women explorers, traders, adventurers, freed slaves, immigrants, fortune hunters, farmers, businessmen, and members of religious sects went west, <u>pushed</u> by events at home and <u>pulled</u> by visions of a better life.

In Part 2, students meet the people who moved west from the 1840s–1880s and identify the "push and pull" factors that influenced their decisions.

DEFINITIONS

Migrate: To move from one place to another.

Immigrate: To move <u>into</u> a country or region.

Emigrate: To move <u>out of</u> a country or region.

ACTIVITIES

Who Went West?

Students read and interpret quotes of people who settled the West. They consider the fact that most good-byes to people back home were permanent. Often, family and friends were never seen again.

MATERIALS

They Went West reproducible (page 26)

BACKGROUND

People traveled to the West for many reasons. Reading the words of some these pioneers will help students gain a deeper understanding of who these people were and why they were willing to leave friends and family for the unknown.

WHAT TO DO

✪ Ask: How many of you have ever moved from one place to another? How did it feel to say good-bye to a familiar place? What did you leave behind when you moved? What do you remember most about the move? What were you looking forward to?

✪ Distribute the reproducible and have students take turns reading excerpts aloud.

Keeping a Journal

✪ Ask students to speculate about why people who traveled west kept journals and why we value those journals today.

✪ Explain that students will be keeping a journal while they study pioneers. The journals will help them understand what they read, organize their thoughts, and think of questions. These will be "public" not private journals. Students will be asked periodically to share a selection of their own choosing with you and with the class.

✪ The first journal assignment is to answer the question, "If at some point in the future you could go to Mars, would you go?" Suggest that students answer these questions in their journal entry:

1. If your answer is no, explain why. What would it take to make you change your mind?

2. If you answered yes, tell what you would take with you. What would you say to those left behind? What would you hope for at the end of the journey?

✪ Give students the following information:

⊙ Human exploration of Mars could take place as early as 2007.

⊙ It takes from seven to eleven months to travel from Earth to Mars, but the planets only line up for optimal travel every 26 months.

⊙ Some of the problems people would face during a trip from Earth to Mars include boredom; inadequate food, water, and medical supplies; homesickness; and uncertainty about the future.

Ask students to date their journal entries and to reread the entries and add comments to their earlier entries.

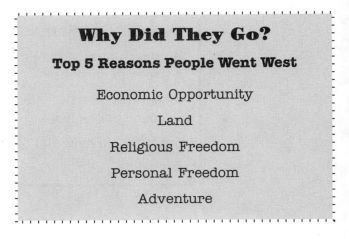

Why Did They Go?

Top 5 Reasons People Went West

Economic Opportunity

Land

Religious Freedom

Personal Freedom

Adventure

Push and Pull

Students learn about "Push/Pull" factors in human migration and, using the reproducible "Push/Pull" Cards, consider some of the reasons people moved west in the 1840s–1880s.

MATERIALS

"Push/Pull" Cards reproducible (page 27) (copy and cut apart)

BACKGROUND

"Push/Pull" is a concept geographers use to explain human migrations. "Push" factors include events or situations that might convince a person to leave home—lack of opportunity to own land, drought, or unemployment. "Pull" factors include the attractive characteristics of an area—economic opportunity (land or jobs), political and religious freedom, favorable climate.

WHAT TO DO

⊗ Define "Push/Pull" as a way of describing the reasons why people migrate from one place to another.

⊗ Post these headings on a bulletin board: Economic Opportunity, Health, Political/Religious Freedom, Adventure. Each Push/Pull Card fits one of these categories.

⊗ Make copies of the "Push/Pull" Cards reproducible and cut the cards apart. Distribute one or more cards to each student. Have students determine whether their card represents "push" or "pull" and in which category, or categories, their card belongs.

⊗ Have students work in groups to find out more about the specific "Push/Pull" events that created the westward migrations of the 1840s. (Some events are listed on page 22.)

	Economic Opp'y	Health	Freedom	Adventure
"PULL" CARDS				
In Oregon I've heard the pigs run around already cooked.	X			
There's gold out there and I'm going to find it.	X			X
It will be less crowded so there will be less illness.		X		
I can practice my religion.			X	
There is no slavery there.			X	
I want to own enough land to support my family.	X			
"PUSH" CARDS				
I cannot live where there is slavery.			X	
I lost everything when the banks closed.	X			
People here are dying of cholera.		X		
We are being persecuted for our religious beliefs.			X	
There is no way for me to own land here.	X			
People here try to limit what I can become.			X	

Pull

Gold and silver

Gold: California 1849–1850's; Colorado 1859; Black Hills of South Dakota 1874

Silver: Nevada 1860

Good farm land

1840s "Oregon Fever"; Homestead Act 1862; railroad made it easier to travel; advertised land for sale after Civil War

Push

Financial collapse

On May 10, 1837, banks closed and people panicked. In the face of economic depression, many people headed west to start over. Another financial panic in 1857 caused many people in the Midwest to head farther west.

Sickness/Epidemics

In the 1830s, a cholera epidemic that had started in Asia and passed through Europe, reached the United States. Twenty years later, people were still dying; 30,000 died in 1850. To escape disease and epidemics in crowded cities, people moved west. They brought cholera with them and infected others, including Indians they came in contact with along the way.

Religious persecution

Mormons, driven out of Illinois in 1846, went west to find a place to practice their religion in peace. Share the information about the Mormons in the Close Ups on page 25 with students.

Slavery

Despite the Emancipation Proclamation, slavery was legal in many states until the end of the Civil War. In the years leading up to the Civil War, people escaping slavery traveled west along with abolitionists (people opposed to slavery on moral grounds) and non-slave-owning farmers who could not compete with slave owners.

EXTEND THE LESSON

Ask students to make a journal entry identifying push/pull influences in their own lives: "I am *pulled* to do x for these reasons; and *pushed* for these reasons."

Go West!

Students will read and discuss tall tales, rumors, and factual information that led to the "Great Emigration" of 1843.

MATERIALS

Believe It or Not reproducible (page 28)

BACKGROUND

Part of what pulled people to the West were myths and stories about the riches and plentiful land to be found there. The stories spread as far as Europe. Steamship companies used them to attract passengers to the United States. Later, railroads would promote the availability of free land on the Great Plains.

In the 1840s, tales of Oregon's riches spurred settlement. Americans felt it was their "manifest destiny" that Oregon Country should belong to the United States and not Great Britain. People acted on the belief that the more American settlers there were in Oregon Country, the stronger was the United States' claim. Tales of gold in California (and later in Colorado, Nevada, and the Black Hills of the Dakotas) enticed many men and families to uproot themselves and head west. After the Civil War, the settlement of the Great Plains was fueled by stories of its agricultural superiority.

WHAT TO DO

⊛ Copy and distribute the reproducible. Ask students why people would believe exaggerated tales about Oregon. (*Because they wanted to, because there was a lack of accurate information about the West.*)

⊛ What economic conditions in the East might have made people more likely to believe these myths? (*Economic depression of 1837; desire for land and economic opportunity*)

⊛ Use information in the Close Up "54° 40' or Fight" on page 25 to point out that people were attracted to Oregon for political reasons.

⊛ Discuss the quotes and questions on the reproducible:

Which of the quotes seems exaggerated? Why? In the poem "Over the Rocky Mountains Height," what does the poet mean by "the living sea"? (*pioneers*) How does the poem (which appeared on the cover of a Guide Book) reassure people who are coming to Oregon? (*by making it clear that lots of other people are headed there, too, and will reach their destination*)

EXTEND THE LESSON

Ask students to identify current myths about the West.

. . . .

Go for the Gold

Students learn what happened after gold was found in California in 1848 and the effect its discovery had on the country, on the forty-niners, and on Native Americans.

MATERIALS

The Gold Rush: Facts and Myths Quick Quiz reproducible (page 29)

BACKGROUND

In 1848–49, as many as 80,000 gold prospectors headed to seek their fortunes in California after hearing that gold had been discovered at Sutter's Mill, near Sacramento. This was the beginning of the California Gold Rush. By the time it ended a few years later (after the easy-to-find gold was exhausted), the prospectors, known as forty-niners, had profoundly changed California and the idea of the West. Of those who struck gold, very few became rich. Most miners earned only a few cents to a few dollars a day for ten or more hours of backbreaking work panning for gold. Much of their earnings went to the stores, saloons, and boarding houses in the mining towns that sprang up around the "diggings." The owners of these businesses made some of the biggest fortunes during the Gold Rush.

The influx of miners from all corners of the world who poured into California by land and sea changed San Francisco from a sleepy town to a booming city. It also had a devastating impact on the 150,000 Native Americans living in California. By 1870, there were only about 30,000 left. Murder, enslavement, and disease resulted in what some historians consider the worst slaughter of Indian people in United States history.

WHAT TO DO

⊛ Copy and distribute The Gold Rush reproducible and give students time to research answers to questions.

⊛ Have students answer the questions.

⊛ Review the following answers and explanations with students.

1. (True) When word got out that gold had been found in the American River, which ran through John Sutter's property, his worst fears came true, and his land was overrun by miners.

2. (True) People pouring into California to mine gold increased pressure to make it a state.

3. (c)

4. (b) San Francisco growth was spurred on by merchants who wanted to "mine the miners" and provide ways for them to spend their money.

5. (True) Miners often gambled away their gold almost as fast as they found it. They also used gold to buy necessities like tools and food and clothing. Merchants who supplied the miners made fortunes.

6. (b) The Native Americans of California posed no threat to the miners—the opposite was true. Miners and others who flooded into the area posed a threat to Native Americans, passively through the spread of disease and actively by rounding up, enslaving, and murdering Native American men, women, and children.

7. (d) Murder, enslavement, and disease resulted in what has been called "the worst slaughter of Indian people in United States history."

8. (False) From the beginning of the Gold Rush, American miners drove most foreigners off claims, especially Mexicans (who, until the Treaty of Guadeloupe Hidalgo in 1846, had governed California) and Chinese. They were persecuted and barred from mining camps.

9. (b) In the early years of the Gold Rush, most miners panned for gold, working alone or in small groups. Some hired or forced others to pan for them. Panning involved backbreaking digging and standing in icy water for many hours. Later, as the surface supply of gold was gathered up, independent miners left or went to work for large mining companies that could afford to use more expensive methods to dig deeper for gold. Only a very few people ever found gold lying around to be picked up.

10. (True) "Gold Fever" for independent miners ended in the mid-1850s when the surface gold was exhausted and gold mining became a big business.

"Gold Fever" didn't die. Each new discovery of gold (and silver) brought a fresh wave of prospectors to the West: to the Gila River area of California in the mid-1850s, to Pikes Peak in Colorado in 1858, to the Comstock lode (gold and silver) in Nevada in 1860, to the Black Hills of the Dakotas in 1874, and to Alaska in the 1890s.

EXTEND THE LESSON

Ask students to write answers to the following questions in their journals: If gold were discovered on Mars, what would happen? Would Congress fund an accelerated space program for Mars exploration? Would the discovery of gold on Mars make it more or less likely that you would want to go there?

Add It Up—How Many Traveled the Trail?

Students calculate the total number of people who traveled west during the peak years of the Oregon and California trails and refer to the Time Line to see what events affected the number of people traveling west.

MATERIALS

How Many Went West? (page 30) and Map of the Oregon and California Trails (page 49) reproducibles; Time Line (page 6)

BACKGROUND

Historians put the number of pioneers traveling west in the years 1841–1866 on the Oregon and California trails at about 350,000. Great surges in numbers corresponded to the aftermath of events in the East and Midwest, such as financial panics, depressions, or war; or events in the West, such as the discoveries of gold and silver or the land made available through the Homestead Act.

WHAT TO DO

⊗ Organize the class in small groups of three or four students. Distribute the reproducible How Many Went West? to each student and a copy of the Time Line to each group. Groups should also be encouraged to use other reference materials.

⊗ Challenge students to establish a connection between events of a specific year and the number of people who headed west that year. Compare dates with numbers traveling the trails.

⊗ Ask: In which years is there a clear connection between events and number of pioneers? (*Students should identify 1849 as the beginning of the Gold Rush, which explains why 30,000 people hit the trail that year and 55,000 in 1850. In 1859 gold was discovered in Pikes Peak and another 30,000 were on the trail. In 1865, after the Civil War ended, 25,000 people moved west, to take advantage of the Homestead Act of 1862.*) For which years is it harder to explain the number of pioneers on the trails?

⊗ Invite students to display the information in the reproducible as a line graph.

EXTEND THE LESSON

Divide the class into two groups, one to do research about the Oregon Trail, and the other to research the California Trail. Have each group report back to the class answering these questions:

1. What motivated people to take this trail to the West?

2. What kind of person took this particular trail?

3. What is left of the trail today?

CLOSE UPS

The Mormons—Pioneers in Search of a Homeland

Finding a place to practice their religion without fear of persecution was the pull that brought the Mormons west. After fleeing from other states to escape the hostility of non-Mormons, John Smith, the founder of the religion, decided Mormons could not be safe within the United States. When Smith was killed by a mob in Illinois, Brigham Young became the leader of the church. He decided that the Mormons should move west to Utah and the Great Salt Lake. (Utah was not part of the United States at that time.) The Great Salt Lake was a remote area surrounded by the Wasatch Mountains—a natural barrier that would serve as a protection from the other settlers.

In 1847, Young and approximately 150 other Mormons started their westward trek. It was a well-planned and highly disciplined migration. Young set rules for everything: when and how far they would travel each day, when they would wake up and go to sleep, and when they would eat meals. He ensured the rules were followed by creating a pyramid of authority. Young also decided that they should steer clear of other westward-bound pioneers—and potential trouble with them—by traveling on a more difficult route, just north of the Oregon Trail. What came to be known as the Mormon Trail traversed rivers, canyons, and mountains. Though some people in that first group of Mormon emigrants contracted diseases, all survived the trip.

The first Mormon pioneers reached the Great Salt Lake in July 1847 determined to farm the land and make the area their home. By 1860, after many more migrations, there were a total of 40,000 residents in over 150 communities.

"54° 40' or Fight"

In the 1830s, Oregon Country, a vast area of the Pacific Northwest claimed by Great Britain was jointly occupied by American and British settlers. As more and more Americans poured into Oregon in the 1840s, pressure built for the entire area to come under the control of the United States. James Polk won the presidential election of 1844 in part because he campaigned using the slogan "54°40' or Fight." He agreed with those who thought that the United States should control all of Oregon Country, all the way to its northernmost border at the 54th parallel (line of latitude). But Great Britain would not yield its claim to all of Oregon Country. The terms of a compromise worked out in 1846 set the boundary of the U.S.-controlled portion of Oregon Country at the 49th parallel, with the British continuing to control the area north of that latitude. Oregon joined the United States as the thirty-third state in 1859.

Find Out More

Look at a world map or globe. Find the 49th and 54th parallels. What other places in the world are on the same latitudes?

THEY WENT WEST

"[T]hey [the emigrants] were men and women who had already made one or more moves before in a restless search for better lands. They were children of parents who themselves had moved to new lands. . . .They had owned land before, had cleared land before, and were prepared to clear and own land again. And they were young. Most of the population that moved across half the continent were between sixteen and thirty-five years of age."

—Lillian Schlissel, *Women's Diaries*

"In the winter of 18 and 46 our neighbor got hold of Fremont's history of California and began talking of moving to the New Country [California] & brought the book for my husband to read, & he was carried away with the idea too. I said, O let us not go…"

Mary A. Jones

—Lillian Schlissel, *Women's Diaries*

"How our friends crowded around us at parting. Some cried and talked of Indians and bears. I was seven years old, had been staying with friends…and they felt so badly about my going west."

Lillie Marcks, on departing Tiffin, Ohio in 1869

—Joanna Stratton, *Pioneer Women*

"To say I wept bitterly would but faintly express the ocean of tears I shed on leaving my beloved home and state to take up residence in the 'wild and woolly West.'. . . .To me it spelled destruction, desperadoes, and cyclones. I could not agree with my husband that any good could come out of such a country."

Mrs. W. B. Caton, describing her feelings about leaving home for Kansas in 1879

—Joanna Stratton, *Pioneer Women*

"I see no class distinction here, not as in Sweden, where the working people are rabble and the lazy gentlemen are called better folk. . . .We are free to move. . . .A man can leave his job any time he wants!. . . .There is room here for all of Sweden's inhabitants."

A Swedish settler

—Meridel Le Sueur, *North Star Country*

"Jane I left you and them boys for no other reason than this to come here to procur a littl property by the swet of my brow so that we could have a place of our own that I mite not be a dog for other people any longer."

An anonymous prospector

—Reader's Digest, *Story of the Great American West*

"Men who could build a railroad to the moon perhaps could build one over these mountains, but I doubt it. . . and it is said the worst is yet to come. But never mind, gold lies ahead."

William Wilson

—Geoffrey C. Ward, *The West*

"PUSH/PULL" CARDS

In Oregon I've heard the pigs run around already cooked.

There's gold out there, and I'm going to find it.

It will be less crowded, so there will be less illness.

I can practice my religion.

There is no slavery there.

I want to own enough land to support my family.

I cannot live where there is slavery.

I lost everything when the banks closed.

People here are dying of cholera.

We are being persecuted for our religious beliefs.

There is no way for me to own land here.

People here try to limit what I can become.

BELIEVE IT OR NOT

Read some of the claims made about Oregon, California, and the Great Plains. Why do you think people would believe such claims?

Oregon

"[In Oregon] the pigs are running about under the great acorn trees, round and fat, and already cooked, with knives and forks sticking in them so that you can cut off a slice whenever you are hungry."

—Time-Life Books, *The Pioneers*

"Oregon cannot be [out]done whether in wheat, oats, rye, barley, buckwheat, peas, beans, potatoes, turnips, cabbages, onions, parsnips, carrots, beets, currants, gooseberries, strawberries, apples, peaches, pears, or fat and healthy babies."

—Time-Life Books, *The Pioneers*

"The soil...is rich beyond comparison. . .. The epidemic [cholera] of the [Midwest] country. . ...is scarcely known here...."

—Lillian Schlissel, *Women's Diaries*

"When improved [by settlers] Oregon will become 'the loveliest and most envied country on earth.'"

—Time-Life Books, *The Pioneers*

"Over the Rocky Mountains height,
Like ocean in its tided might,
The living sea rolls onward, on!
And onward on, the stream shall pour
And reach the far Pacific shore,
And fill the plains of Oregon."

—Poem on the cover of *The National Wagon Road Guide*, San Francisco, 1858

"Come! All men are free and equal before the law. Religious freedom is absolute and there is not the slightest connection between church and state."

—Advertisement for Oregon in Europe, 1847

California

"[Riverbeds] are paved with gold to the thickness of a hand. . .. [T]wenty to fifty thousand dollars of gold. . . [can] be picked out almost instantly."

—*Emigrant's Guide to the Gold Mines*

"Fortune lies abroad upon the surface of the earth as plentiful as mud in our streets."

—Horace Greeley in the *New York Daily Tribune*

Great Plains

"The PLAINS are not deserts, but the OPPOSITE, and the. . .basis of the future empire."

—Time-Life Books, *The Pioneers*

The railroads permanently changed the weather and brought more rain to the Great Plains.

—Popular belief in 1870s and early 1880s (a period of unusually heavy rainfall and bumper crops for farmers on the Plains)

Name_____ Date_____

THE GOLD RUSH
Facts and Myths Quick Quiz

Take this quiz to find out how much you know about the Gold Rush.

1. The man on whose property gold was first discovered in California in 1848 tried to keep it a secret.

      True   or   False

2. California's population rose from 20,000 in 1848 to 220,000 in 1852 when it became a state.

      True   or   False

3. Mining in California during the gold rush increased the world's supply of gold by _____.

      (a) 10%

      (b) 33%

      (c) more than 100%

4. The population of San Francisco rose from 2,000 in 1849 to 30,000 in 1850 in part because:

      (a) there was free housing in the city.

      (b) San Francisco was the seaport entry point through which many miners passed on their way to and from the gold fields.

      (c) gold was found under the city streets.

5. More people in California got rich by selling to miners than by finding gold.

      True   or   False

6. The most deadly threat to the forty-niners was _____.

      (a) hostile Native American tribes

      (b) cholera

      (c) rattlesnakes

7. The population of Native Americans in California fell from 150,000 in 1848 to 30,000 in 1870 because of _____.

      (a) disease

      (b) enslavement

      (c) murder

      (d) all three

8. Foreigners, especially Chinese and Mexicans, worked peacefully side by side with American miners in the gold fields.

      True   or   False

9. Most Forty-niners found gold by

      (a) tunneling into mountainsides with heavy machinery.

      (b) washing pans of sand to separate out the heavier gold-bearing sand.

      (c) picking it up off the ground.

10. "Gold Fever" ended when gold mining in California became big business.

      True   or   False

HOW MANY WENT WEST?

The table below gives estimates of how many people traveled on the Oregon and California trails between 1841 and 1866.

1841	**60**
1842	**200**
1843	**1,000**
1844	**4,000**
1845	**5,000**
1846	**1,000**
1847	**2,000**
1848	**4,000**
1849	**30,000**
1850	**55,000**
1851	**10,000**
1852	**50,000**
1853	**20,000**
1854	**10,000**
1855	**5,000**
1856	**5,000**
1857	**5,000**
1858	**10,000**
1859	**30,000**
1860	**15,000**
1861	**5,000**
1862	**5,000**
1863	**10,000**
1864	**20,000**
1865	**25,000**
1866	**25,000**
Total 1841–1866:	**352,260**

History Comes Alive Teaching Unit: Pioneers   Scholastic Professional Books

Part 3

ON THE TRAIL
1840s–1850s

INTRODUCTION

Oregon Fever hit in the early 1840s. It was 2,400 miles from Independence, Missouri, to Oregon's lush Willamette Valley. In 1843 the first large wagon train left: 120 wagons with 1,000 pioneers on board. Going to Oregon at that time meant leaving the United States; Oregon did not become a U.S. Territory until 1848. In the 1840s alone, 34,000 died along the trail from cholera, accidents, lightning, hunger, or overwork. Historians have calculated that there was one pioneer grave for every 80 yards of the Oregon Trail. The grueling trip took six to eight months. Pioneers tried to leave in April and travel 10 to 20 miles a day in order to reach Oregon before winter.

This section introduces students to the preparations and challenges of a covered wagon trip on the Oregon and California trails. Students learn what pioneers needed to know when they arrived in Independence, Missouri, or other jumping off places for the trails west. They calculate the expense of provisions and determine whether a horse, ox, or mule was the best investment for pulling a wagon.

ACTIVITIES

Are You a Greenhorn?

Students learn what pioneers on the Oregon and California trails needed to know to survive the trip.

MATERIAL

Greenhorn Guidebook reproducible (page 40)

BACKGROUND

Pioneers with little or no experience of the West were known as "greenhorns." Their best hope for a successful journey to Oregon or the California gold fields was to travel with an experienced guide. Guidebooks were advertised as the next best thing, and soon, emigrants had dozens to choose from. However, the information in guidebooks was often out of date, and pioneers using them were disastrously misinformed about the journey.

WHAT TO DO

✸ Explain the concept of "greenhorn" and point out to students that knowledge of pioneering skills sometimes made the difference between surviving the trip and dying along the way. Pioneers could gain some knowledge from guidebooks and from the advice of experienced travelers.

✸ Copy and distribute the Greenhorn Guidebook. Go over *The Prairie Traveler* guidebook entries and the glossary of terms.

✸ Have students take the "Do You Know How To…?" quiz (Greenhorn Guidebook, page 40) and look for answers to the questions in source books and on Web sites (see Resources, page 73).

✸ Go over the answers to the quiz:

"DO YOU KNOW HOW TO…?"

1. Pack eggs and china plates so they will not break on a rough wagon journey? *(Pack breakables in a barrel of cornmeal or flour.)*

2. Keep meat from spoiling on the journey? *(Cut meat in strips and dry it over a fire or in the sun.)*

3. Make a fire without wood? *(Use dried buffalo "chips" [dung] for an odorless fire.)*

4. Make a fire in a windy spot? *(Dig a trench and start the fire in the bottom to protect it from the wind.)*

5. Help a lame ox to keep moving? *(Make a leather drawstring "shoe" to put over the ox's hoofs.)*

6. Find your way back to the trail if you get lost? *(Trails often ran along a river. If lost, you could find the river by following buffalo tracks.)*

7. Get a message from home—or send one back—while on the trail? *(You could leave a letter at a fort along the trail to be carried east by a returning traveler. People back home could send a letter to one of the forts to await your arrival.)*

8. Identify poisonous alkali water? *(Look for yellowish-red grass growing around a spring. Keep oxen, mules, and horses away from both grass and water at the site.)*

9. Get your wagon across a deep river? *(Waterproof the wagon and float it across.)*

Stocking Up

Students learn about the practical, and often difficult, decisions pioneers faced when packing for the long trip west.

MATERIALS

Pack Your Bags reproducible (page 41); *at least one pound each* of rice, dried beans, flour, and cornmeal; resealable plastic bags; plastic containers of different sizes; scale; freeze-dried camping foods; bushel basket (if available)

BACKGROUND

Pioneers needed to purchase food, tools, clothing, and other supplies before leaving Independence, Missouri, for the trail west, but these things were not cheap. It cost $700 to $1,500 (about five years' wages!) to launch a family across the continent. As more and more travelers headed west, merchants flocked to Independence and other jumping off points in Missouri to sell food, wagons, oxen, mules, horses, and other supplies to the pioneers.

WHAT TO DO

✸ Show students the modern-day, freeze-dried foods for camping. Discuss why food is produced and packaged that way and what, as pioneers, they would have had to consider when buying supplies. Lead them to compile a list of considerations about what they'd pack, such as *How useful would a given item be? Would it take up too much space? Would it be too heavy to haul? Where would it fit in the wagon?* and so on. Discuss that such considerations inevitably meant that pioneers had to leave behind things they cared about.

✸ Show students the bags of flour, cornmeal, rice, and dried beans. Ask them to estimate the weight of each package. Then ask them to guess how much of each item pioneers would need to bring. Have them compare their estimates to the amounts on page 41.

Invite them to design ways to carry package the food so it would take up as little room as possible. They can use bags or plastic containers.

✸ Discuss the answers they gave to the question on the reproducible. (*Students may suggest household items, furniture for the new home, school books, mending tools, or toys.*)

✸ Ask: How did pioneers supplement the foods they brought with them? (*buying or trading for food along the way, hunting and fishing, picking berries, fruits, and plants*)

EXTEND THE LESSON

Ask students to bring into class something that holds memories for them and explain why they would not leave it behind if they had to move.

Mules, Oxen, Horses

Students make a spinner showing different characteristics of each animal and its relative merits for the trip west.

MATERIALS

plain paper, brass fasteners, scissors, markers

BACKGROUND

One of the most important decisions pioneers had to make before setting off was which animals they would purchase to pull their wagons. Horses weren't as strong as oxen or mules and therefore couldn't haul as much. Horses also were at risk of being stolen. But once out west, pioneers would want horses for personal transportation or to carry packs. Oxen were strong and cheaper than mules or horses, but their split hooves could be a problem on certain parts of the trail. On the other hand, in desperate times, they could be killed and eaten. Mules were more expensive to buy and feed than oxen, but they could travel faster and were sure-footed on terrain oxen were not.

WHAT TO DO

⊛ Discuss what pioneers needed in a draft animal: strength to pull a heavy load and the ability to live on grass and food available along the route.

⊛ Distribute copies of the spinner chart (*right*) and materials needed to put spinners together. Model how to cut the plain paper into a circular cover with a triangular window. Have students construct their spinners and decorate the cover with drawings.

⊛ Now read students the following quote from Captain Marcy's *The Prairie Traveler* (see the Greenhorn Guidebook, page 40). Explain that you will pause and ask for volunteers to fill in the blanks in the paragraph based on the information on their spinners. (Be careful not to read the answers, which appear in brackets.)

"There has been much discussion regarding the relative merits of mules and oxen for prairie traveling, and the question is yet far from being settled. Upon good firm roads, in a populated country, where grain could be procured, I should unquestionably give the preference to_____ [mules], as they travel faster and endure the summer heat much better than _____ [oxen]. When the march is to extend 1500 to 2000 miles, or over a rough, sandy or muddy road, I believe young ____[oxen] will perform better than ____[mules].... ____[Oxen] are much less likely to be stampeded and driven off by Indians....____[Oxen] can if necessary be used for [food]."

⊛ Ask students why they think Captain Marcy did not include horses in this comparison.

EXTEND THE LESSON

Assign teams to find out more about traveling the western trails with mules and oxen.

Mules
Travel fast (20 miles/day) on hard-packed trails
Can endure heat
Best on journeys up to 1,000 miles
Expensive to feed; more expensive to buy than oxen
Can be stampeded or stolen
Drown if they get water in their ears

Oxen
Not likely to be stampeded or stolen
Split hooves a problem on some terrain
Slow moving (15 miles/day)
Cheap to feed—eat prairie grasses
Can be used as food
Cheapest means of transportation
Good for long journeys—1,500 to 2,000 miles

Horses
More expensive than oxen or mules
Likely to be stolen—very desirable
For riding usually; rarely used to pull heavy wagons
Need more feed to work
Expensive to feed

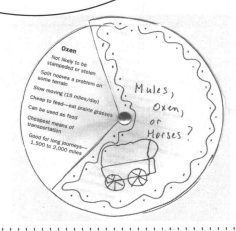

Inside a Covered Wagon

Students determine the size of covered wagons used on the Oregon and California trails and consider how they were packed and waterproofed.

MATERIALS

Covered Wagon Cross Section reproducible (page 42), masking tape, cardboard box, small child's wagon (optional)

BACKGROUND

Pioneers on the Oregon and California trails used ordinary farm wagons (vehicles they were used

34

to) and added a framework of bent hickory bows across the wagon bed. Over the framework they stretched a canvas covering to protect them and their belongings. The canvas cover had draw-strings on the ends which could be pulled tight to close up the wagon and loosened to open it, and it was treated with linseed oil to make it water-proof. On the inside of the cover, pioneer women sewed pockets for carrying small items. With wooden, spoked wheels and iron "tires," the cov-ered wagon was ready to roll. Tools and spare parts were lashed to the outside of the wagon. Often a cow or cows were tied on behind the wagon to provide a supply of milk and butter for the travelers. Everyone who could, walked.

WHAT TO DO

⊛ Distribute Covered Wagon Cross Section and discuss the different parts of the wagon.

⊛ On the classroom floor or on a playground, have students tape off one or more areas four feet wide and ten to twelve feet long to show the interior dimensions of a typical wagon. (These wagons were fairly small. The side rail-ings were about 2 feet high; above that curved a framework covered with canvas. The inside "roof" was usually about five feet above the wagon bed at its highest point. A fully loaded wagon could carry up to 2,500 pounds.)

⊛ Students calculate both the area inside the covered wagon (they'll have to approximate, accounting for the diminishing space toward the sides) and how many boxes the size of the cardboard one could fit inside.

⊛ Ask a small group of students to research and report on the process of sealing a wagon so it could be floated across deep rivers. Other stu-dents can sew pockets to one side of a sheet to show how the inside of the wagon cover was used for storage.

EXTEND THE LESSON

Ask students to compare the journeys of pio-neers on the Oregon Trail to the journeys of future travelers to Mars. Make sure they under-stand that one important difference is that the pioneers on the Oregon Trail were not passen-gers in any sense of the word. Except for infants

and very sick people, for most of the journey everybody walked.

· ·

On the Trail

Students learn about the organization and daily schedule of a six-month trip on the Oregon trail. Through firsthand accounts and a read-aloud play, they learn about the illnesses, hazards, and difficulties pioneers faced along the way.

MATERIALS

Letters Home, A Read-Aloud Play reproducibles (pages 43–46); *Westward Bound, 1849* repro-ducibles (pages 47–48); Map of the Oregon and California Trails reproducible (page 49); road map of the United States

BACKGROUND

What we know about the experiences of pioneers on the Oregon and California trails comes from pioneers' journals, written by the light of cooking fires while their wagon trains were halted for a rest. Exhausted and hungry, often sick and cold, men and women picked up their pens to record how many miles they had come that day; what the trail conditions were like; what food they had or wished they had; who had died or been injured; and, sometimes, how they felt about the journey. Many pioneers kept journals because they knew they were taking part in an important historical movement and wanted to leave a record of it for their families. Pioneer journals became treasured family keepsakes, and many eventually found their way into libraries and historical archives.

The play *Letters Home*, an excerpt from which is included here, consists of fictional let-ters based on actual journal entries, letters, and reminiscences of pioneers who traveled the Oregon Trail. *Westward Bound, 1849* is a selec-tion from the diary of Samuel Murray Stover, a forty-niner, who traveled from Tennessee to California in search of gold. Up to and through South Pass, in present-day Wyoming, the home-steaders' and gold hunters' trails were the same. There they went their separate ways, Oregon-bound pioneers facing the crossing of the Cascade Mountains or rafting down the Columbia River, Forty-niners on the California Trail heading toward scorching deserts and the Sierra Nevada Mountains.

WHAT TO DO

⊗ Divide the class into small groups of four or five students.

⊗ Distribute to each group one copy of the *Letters Home*: *Westward Bound, 1849*; and map reproducibles. Explain that the play is fictional but based on actual letters, and the diary entries were made by Samuel Murray Stover in 1849 on his way to the gold "diggings" in California. His descendants published his diary in the 1930s. The entries included here represent a small portion of the whole diary. Explain also that actual letters, unlike the fictional ones of the play, would not have been sent individually but saved up and left at one of the forts along the trail to be passed along to someone returning east.

⊗ Have each group prepare a comparison of the two journeys. First ask them to create a chart with these topic headings: Animals; Weather; Wagons; Dangers/Fears; Illness/Death; Indians; Food/Hunger; Landmarks; and Other Pioneers on the Trail. Then have them take turns entering the dates of the letters or diary entries that mention those topics. Students should use the map to locate landmarks mentioned in the diary and letters.

Animals
    Letters: 3/18; 5/10; 5/16; 6/6; 6/10;
        6/17; 6/20; 7/23; 8/3
    Diary: 6/1; 6/16; 7/24; 8/23; 8/26
Weather
    Letters: 5/16; 6/10
    Diary: 6/13
Wagons
    Letters: 3/18; 6/6; 6/10; 6/22; 7/6;
        10/2; 10/5 (writer 8)
    Diary: 7/15
Dangers/Fears
    Letters: 6/22; 10/19
    Diary: 6/13
Illness/Death
    Letters: 6/6; 6/20; 7/23; 10/19
    Diary: 6/1; 7/15; 8/23; 8/26

Indians
    Letters: 3/18; 6/10; 7/10
    Diary: 6/1
Food/Hunger
    Letters: 6/17; 10/19
    Diary: 7/24; 9/12
Landmarks
    Letters: 7/10; 7/25; 8/3
    Diary: 6/24; 8/31
Other Pioneers on the Trail
    Letters: 5/10
    Diary: 7/15

⊗ Ask students which category has the most entries and why. (*Animals. Animals were the key to the success of the pioneers' journey; finding food and water for them and keeping them healthy was very important. Wild animals were a source of food.*)

⊗ Ask volunteers to read aloud one or more letters or diary entries for each topic.

⊗ In their own journals, ask students to write three entries as if they were traveling on the Oregon Trail. The dates and places described should reflect the most favorable time of year for the trip and show an understanding of how fast a typical wagon train traveled. On their maps students can mark the places they mention in their entries; they can invent their own symbols, explained in keys, that indicate what each place is or what they experienced there (for example, an *x* could mean *buffalo crossing*, and a picture of a wagon wheel could mean *other pioneers*).

EXTEND THE LESSON

Compare the routes shown on Map of the Oregon and California Trails with a current road map of the United States. Ask: Do today's highways follow the pioneer trails? Have students calculate how long a trip from Independence, Missouri, to the Columbia River or to Davis, California, would take today. They should assume travel is by car at 55 mph.

Walk the Trail

Students discover what it feels like to walk a mile and calculate the number of steps in 2,000 miles.

MATERIALS

Map of the Oregon and California Trails reproducible (page 49); current U.S. road map; stopwatch; pedometer (optional)

BACKGROUND

Most people walked the entire length of the Oregon and California trails. The exceptions were people who could afford a horse and the very old or very young, who rode uncomfortably in wagons without springs. The goal of a wagon train was to cover 20 miles a day; 10 to 13 miles was the usual distance achieved.

WHAT TO DO

⊗ Students calculate how many times they would have to walk around the school's track or playground to experience just the distance of one day's travel on the Oregon Trail (treated for this purpose as 15 miles). They can then walk a mile (or more) and describe the experience in their journals. Have them time their mile and multiply the time by 15 to find out how long it would take to walk 15 miles. (Ask students to add in at least one hour for rest and food, which the pioneers called "nooning," during the hypothetical 15-mile walk.)

⊗ In addition, challenge students to do the 15 miles (over several days or weeks). Make a "Walk the Trail Log" with headings such as Date, Time, Distance Walked, and Total Distance So Far.

⊗ Ask students to calculate how many steps they would have to take to walk 2,000 miles. To determine the length of each student's step, have them work in pairs. The first student takes a normal step and holds it while the partner measures the distance between the heel of the front foot and the heel of the back foot. Students then determine the number of their steps in a mile by dividing the

number of inches in a mile (63,360) by the length in inches of their steps. To find out how many steps it would take to walk 2,000 miles, they multiply the answer by 2,000.

⊗ Students can use a current map of the U.S. to identify the present-day states the Oregon and California trails passed through. Point out that the trail was miles wide at some points because pioneers spread out in search of water and grass.

EXTEND THE LESSON

Ask students to imagine they are walking a mile (or several miles) on the Oregon or California trails and to record in their journals where they are and what they see along the way: natural wonders; physical features of the terrain; forts; weather; and so on.

Invite students to share their journal entries with the class.

Along the Way: Wildlife and Landmarks

Students gain an appreciation for animals that pioneers encountered on their way west, including buffalo, antelope, and prairie dogs (which particularly amused the children). Students also learn about landmarks pioneers looked for along the Oregon Trail—Courthouse Rock, Chimney Rock, Independence Rock, South Pass, Soda Springs, and others. (Many pioneers wrote their names and comments on Independence Rock.)

MATERIALS

Map of California and Oregon Trails reproducible (page 49);, Prairie Dog Pop-up reproducible (page 50) index cards; tape; colored markers; scissors; white paper, permanent black ink; water; brown water color; and paint brushes

BACKGROUND

Along the trails, pioneers encountered animals on the journey that most had never seen before:

antelope, grizzly and black bears, coyotes, rattlesnakes, buffalo, and prairie dogs. Many animals, familiar and unfamiliar, were hunted for food, hides, or sport; others, like prairie dogs, provided interest and amusement for the weary pioneers. Bears and rattlesnakes were dangers to be treated with respect.

WHAT TO DO

⊗ Invite students to volunteer to become experts on a species of animal found on the Great Plains or in the Rocky Mountains. The experts will report back to the class about the animal's size, habitat, behavior, eating habits, and current status (such as *endangered*).

⊗ Prairie dogs were small Great Plains mammals that fascinated the pioneers. Introduce them by reading the following excerpt from *Dakota in the Morning*, in which seven-year-old Bub Sibley, headed for Dakota Territory with his family, gets his first glimpse of a prairie dog "city."

All of a sudden, something seemed to be stirring in the grass not far off....As they approached it...[the entire] city woke to life. Amid a cluster of small mounds that were visible when he looked close, the residents appeared one after another. A score or more little prairie dogs. He watched them pop up out of their houses burrowed below.... Sitting erect, they turned on their haunches, forepaws crossed beneath their chins. ...The small round faces wore twinkling smiles, almost human, looking in pride over their ancient town. He was sure that one of them bowed to him....

—William Harlowe Briggs, *Dakota in the Morning*, Farrar & Rinehart, Inc., 1942

⊗ Explain that a prairie dog "city" was a collection of underground chambers, marked on the surface by dirt mounds with openings on top, that might cover as many as 500 acres. The prairie dogs would sit outside and watch travelers approach. When a human visitor got too close, or some other danger threatened, the prairie dogs would pop down their holes to safety.

⊗ Distribute copies of the Prairie Dog Pop-Up to each student and make the other materials available. After students have completed their prairie dogs, give the signal for students to pop up their prairie dogs, turning the classroom into a prairie dog village.

⊗ Have students use the map of the trails to locate landmarks such as Chimney Rock and South Pass. To show their understanding of the significance of particular animals and landmarks, and of the basic timeline of the trip, ask students to write letters as pioneers on the trail, describing an animal and a landmark and pretending they saw them on two different dates.

⊗ Students can make their letters look authentically old by rewriting them as follows: copy over the letter in permanent ink on one side of a sheet of white paper; gently crumple the letter and dip it in water; then remove the excess water and spread the paper flat. Finally, brush it with a light brown water color wash and let it dry.

EXTEND THE LESSON

Ask students to choose one landmark on the Oregon Trail and write about its condition and status today.

CLOSE UP

The Donner Party—Doomed Pioneers

The fateful journey of the Donner Party began calmly in May, 1846, when members of the Donner and Reed families left Springfield, Illinois, and headed for Independence, Missouri, the start of the Oregon Trail. When the group reached Independence, they joined a wagon train of pioneers who were going to Sutter's Fort in California. The trip was uneventful until the caravan reached Fort Bridger, in present-day Wyoming, in July, 1846. That's where 87 men, women, and children, including the Donners and Reeds, separated from the rest of the group to take a "shortcut" called the Hastings Cutoff.

The new route took the pioneers on a time-consuming trek through the rugged Wasatch Mountains and across the desert. The delays were disastrous. The pioneers who thought the cutoff would save time did not reach the base of the Sierra Nevada mountains until late October. They were soon snowbound on the eastern side of the mountains with little food. Fifteen people attempted to cross the mountains to get help during the winter. Only half of them made their destination, Sutter's Fort, and then bad weather delayed the return of a rescue party for months.

It wasn't until April, 1847, that the last survivors were brought out of the Sierra Nevadas. They had endured the death of family members as well as sickness and starvation. To survive, some of the living pioneers ate the bodies of those who had died. Of the 87 who took the Hastings Cutoff, 45 died.

GREENHORN GUIDEBOOK

"Travel, travel, travel; nothing else will take you to the end of your journey; nothing is wise that does not help you along; nothing is good for you that causes a moment's delay."
— Marcus Whitman, from *The Prairie Traveler* by Randolph B. Marcy, Captain, U.S. Army (1859)

WHEN TO LEAVE (pages 7–8)

Many persons who have had much experience in prairie traveling prefer leaving the Missouri River in March or April, and feeding grain to their animals until the new grass appears. ...The grass, after the 1st of May, is good and abundant upon this road as far as the South Pass [through the Rocky Mountains], from whence there is a section of about 50 miles where it is scarce... As large numbers of cattle pass over the road annually, they soon consume all the grass in these barren localities, and such as pass late in the season are likely to suffer greatly, and oftentimes perish from starvation....

Upon the head of the Sweetwater River, and west of the South Pass, alkaline springs are met with, which are exceedingly poisonous to cattle and horses. They can readily be detected by the yellowish-red color of the grass growing around them. Animals should never be allowed to graze near them or drink the water.

CROSSING RIVERS (page 85)

Mules are good swimmers unless they happen...to get water in their ears, when they are often drowned.

DO YOU KNOW HOW TO...?

1. Pack eggs and china plates so they will not break on a rough wagon journey?

2. Keep meat from spoiling on the journey?

3. Make a fire without wood?

4. Make a fire in a windy spot?

5. Help a lame ox keep moving?

6. Find your way back to the trail if you get lost?

7. Get a message from home—or send one back—while on the trail?

8. Identify poisonous alkali water?

9. Get your wagon across a deep river?

Trail Talk

Meeting the Elephant—having bad luck or accidents on the trail; an unusual or unexpected experience on the journey

Nooning—midday halt for food and rest for people and animals

Oregon—French for hurricane

Nebraska—flat and shallow

Sowbelly—bacon

Slam Johns, Flap Jacks—pancakes

Prairie—French for "large meadow"

To Pan Out—to succeed; gold miners' expression from panning for gold

Tipi—in Sioux, ti means "dwelling"; pi means "used for."

PACK YOUR BAGS

What would you pack for a six-month trip? Here's what an average family brought for their journey to the West.

Food

(For each adult)

200 lbs. flour
300 lbs. of pilot bread
150 lbs. bacon
10 lbs. rice
1/2 bu corn meal
5 lbs. coffee
2 lbs. tea
20 lbs. sugar
1/2 bu dry fruit
10 lbs. salt
baking soda
dried beef
dried beans
molasses
pepper
vinegar

Supplies

(For each family)

wagon
spare wagon parts
(e.g., axles, wheel
rims)
tools
clothing
bedding
axe
guns
cooking utensils
4–6 yoke of oxen
(2 oxen = 1 yoke)
milk cows

Trail Facts
Cost of the trip to Oregon on the Oregon Trail:

$700–$1,500 (about five years' wages in the 1840s)

No matter how much food they started with, by the end of the journey most people were hungry.

What other items might pioneers have brought with them?

_____

_____

_____

_____

Name _____

Date _____

COVERED WAGON CROSS SECTION

A typical covered wagon was four feet wide and ten feet long. It could hold about 2,500 pounds of food and supplies.

Letters Home
A READ-ALOUD PLAY

CAST

ANNIE: Girl traveling along the Oregon Trail

JOEY: Annie's older brother

8 WRITERS

MA: Annie and Joey's mother

DAD: Annie and Joey' father

WAGON MASTER

TOWNSPEOPLE: Non-speaking roles

CAPTAIN: Leader of wagon train

MEMBERS OF WAGON TRAIN

WALTER JAMES: Fiddle player

INDIANS

TRAPPERS

MERCHANTS

Scene. 1850. Along the Oregon Trail. ANNIE and JOEY sit in chairs in the middle of the stage.

(The play is told in the form of letters written by ANNIE, JOEY, and other WRITERS. The WRITERS, with the rest of the non-speaking cast, will appear behind ANNIE and JOEY throughout the play and pantomime the action as the letters are read aloud. When WRITERS speak, they should step forward to stand beside ANNIE and JOEY.)

ANNIE: January 3, 1850

Dear Grandma,

Guess what, Grandma, we might be going to Oregon. Dad read a book about the West, and Ma says he's caught "Oregon fever." The book said Oregon was the Land of Milk and Honey, like that place in the Bible, I forget its name. Ma doesn't want to go. It takes months to get there, and she says what if her and Pa should die on the way, what would happen to us kids? Also, she doesn't want to give up our possessions that mean so much. You can't carry much in those wagons. You know that beautiful sideboard you gave us?

Well, we couldn't take it. We couldn't even take our beds.

Dad says, look at it this way. Land is getting expensive here in Missouri. Joey would never be able to afford a farm of his own when he grows up. But in Oregon, the land is free. All you have to do is get there.

I don't know, but I think I agree with Ma. I don't want to go. Mainly because Ma says, if we went, we'd probably never see you again.

Love, Annie

JOEY: March 18, 1850

Dear Grandma,

It's decided, Grandma, we're going to Oregon! I think we're leaving in May. See, at that time the prairie grasses will have grown tall enough to feed the animals, and we'll get across the Rocky Mountains before winter. The Rocky Mountains, imagine that, Grandma. We're going to see Indians too! We'll be crossing right over their land. Dad says they usually don't mind as long as you don't stop. He says they like to trade. Boy, would I like to have a pony.

Last week Dad and I went to buy a

wagon. They call them "prairie schooners" because the white canvas tops look like sails on boats. We also bought eight oxen to pull it. I hoped we could get horses, but Dad says horses aren't strong enough to pull the wagon over the mountains.

Maybe you could come to Oregon with us.

Love, Joey

JOEY: May 10, 1850

Dear Grandma,

I'm sorry I didn't get to write sooner, but I've been learning to drive oxen. I'm a teamster. It's a lot of responsibility.

You should see us, Grandma. There are 90 wagons in our train. That's hundreds of people going west in our wagon train alone! A lot of wagons broke down during the first week, so we didn't get too far. Ours didn't break down. Now we're making about ten miles a day, the Captain says. I'll bet if you could see us from a bird's eye, we'd look like a great fleet of ships crossing the prairie. There are a lot of children Annie's age and some my age. We're both making new friends. This is the most fun I've ever had!

Love, Joey

ANNIE: May 16, 1850

Dear Grandma,

We're on the Great Plains now. There are no trees at all, nothing but grass as far as you can see. I don't like this place, Grandma. It's terribly hot, 100 degrees all day. We all suffer with it, but I think the animals suffer most of all. We're all exhausted and we haven't even seen the mountains yet. How can we keep this up? Yet just when we think we can't, we see something beautiful. Like yesterday, we passed a giant field of purple wild flowers, it must have been five miles across. It was the most beautiful thing I've ever seen. I'll try to write more later, but my ink is drying up. I miss you.

Love, Annie

JOEY: June 6, 1850

Dear Grandma,

Most people, except the real young and the real old, walk beside the wagons all day. Even people who have horses walk so as to save the animals for when we get to Oregon. Remember our ox, Spot? Well, he dropped dead yesterday. We all cried. We pulled out of line long enough to butcher him. He was a good ox, but he was tough, though.

We stop for lunch at noon, but nobody unpacks the wagon to cook. We eat jerky standing up or sitting down in the shade of the wagons, if we can find any.

Love, Joey

ANNIE: June 10, 1850

Dear Grandma,

We've been traveling along the Platte River. The Platte must be the foulest tasting river in the West. Nobody can stand it, so we make it into coffee before we drink it. Even the animals drink coffee.

The midday heat makes me stupid. We plod and creak along the ruts made by earlier wagon trains until about 7:00. And then we circle the wagons, a great big circle about half the size of Independence, Missouri. We've gotten so good at it now that the last wagon perfectly completes the circle. We put the animals inside the circle so they don't wander off. People say it's also because of Indian attacks, but we haven't seen any Indians yet. Personally, I think the Indians have more sense than to live out here.

Love, Annie

JOEY: June 17, 1850

Dear Grandma,

Dad and I take care of the animals, while Ma and Annie cook dinner—Spot again tonight, but we're running out of Spot. The sunsets are beautiful, like the sun's saying, "Keep moving. It's even more beautiful out west."

Remember Walter James, who worked for

44

the blacksmith? Turns out he plays the fiddle. It sure is sweet listening to his music before we go to bed. It doesn't matter that he can't play all the notes.

Love, Joey

ANNIE: June 20, 1850

Dear Grandma,

There's a lot of death out here. It's hard to get used to. Every day we pass graves and the skeletons of oxen, cows, and horses bleached white by the sun. I didn't know there would be so much death. Yesterday I saw a long braid of black woman's hair tangled in the grass. There was still a comb in it. There's no wood to make coffins, so people bury their dead as best they can. Wild animals dig up the bodies and eat them. I have nightmares about being pulled from my grave, but at least we've had only two deaths so far, and the Captain thought they would have died even if they'd stayed home.

Cholera, they say, is the worst. I hope we don't have any of that.

Love, Annie

WRITER 1: June 22, 1850:

Today, 460 miles from where we started, we crossed the North Fork of the Platte River. It has a cantankerous reputation. Sometimes it's a half mile wide and six inches deep, but for us, it was deeper than a horse's head. We removed the wheels and made flat-bottom boats out of the wagons. Not good boats, but at least they floated. We were aided in this by the Captain, who showed us how to nail buffalo skins over the bottom of the wagon box to make it watertight. We lost not a single wagon. In fact, this crossing that we feared became a day of merriment and relief, which was a blessing, because everyone's getting tired.

WRITER 2: July 2, 1850

Since we crossed the Platte, the land has tilted against us. We climbed for three days steady to a crest beyond which the land dropped into a deep valley. The wonderful thing about this valley was that at its bottom, there were trees! Shade. We haven't seen trees—or their shade—for almost two months. But first we had to get down the hill.

WRITER 3: July 6, 1850

We chained the wagon wheels so they couldn't turn, then with ropes we skidded the wagons down the hill. We lost five wagons when their ropes snapped. Their owners watched with unbelieving eyes as their homes tumbled end over end, disintegrating into splinters. The rest of us accommodated the homeless and their goods as best we could. They won't be left behind, anyway.

WRITER 4: July 10, 1850

We reached Fort Laramie two days ago, and I look forward to leaving. There are friendly Indians, wild fur trappers, and hostile merchants. One fellow, who wears a brace of pistols in his belt and a gold front tooth, makes his living by following the wagon trains up the steep trail to come. He collects the belongings emigrants discard to lighten their loads, and brings them back to Fort Laramie to sell. If we have to abandon something, I'm going to bury it so this scoundrel can't profit from our loss.

ANNIE: July 23, 1850

Dear Grandma,

Everyone's animals are dying now with regularity. I feel sad for them. They came so far, tried so hard, but they didn't make it. I hope no one has reason to say the same about us.

Love, Annie

JOEY: July 25, 1850

Dear Grandma,

We crossed the Continental Divide today! Now all the rivers flow west. We'd heard so much about South Pass that I expected towering cliffs and deep gorges and things, but it turned out to be a gentle meadow. We crossed easily, and now we're at the eastern edge of the Oregon Territory.

You know what Dad said to me this morning? He said, "Son, you've grown up on this trip. It's time to stop to calling you Joey."

Love, Joseph

WRITER 5: August 3, 1850

We've reached Fort Bridger. We traded our poor worn out oxen and some money for fresh oxen. That's how Jim Bridger makes money. He'll take our team, rest them up in good pasture, and then trade them to the next wagon train. They call these animals "recruited oxen." I wish I could recruit a new body for myself. Mine's about done in.

WRITER 6: September 1, 1850

We've made friends we'll never forget, but now they're gone. We almost changed our minds and went to California with the others after hearing how the men at Fort Hall raved about California as the Promised Land. And they told us how dreadful the trail to Oregon would get. Then the Captain explained that those men work for the Hudson's Bay Company, and their furs come from Oregon, so of course they don't want it settled by farmers like us. Live and learn.

JOEY: October 2, 1850

Dear Grandma,

No sooner, it seems, do we cross one range than another rears up before us. We have to stop to push great boulders aside or chop through brush and trees. Sometimes we have to unload all the wagons, and us men pull them up the trail by ropes. We load them up again, go a half mile, and do it all over. As a result we cover no more than three miles a day. Everyone pitches in to help each other, though, and we feel good about that.

Love, Joseph

WRITER 7: October 5, 1850

We must make a decision now. How to get across the Cascade Mountains? We hear about a new wagon route—

WRITER 8:

But it is said to be steep and broken. The other alternative is by water. We'd abandon our wagons and build rafts or boats and float right down the Columbia River...

JOEY: October 19, 1850

Dear Grandma,

We've been riding the Columbia River for two weeks now. It's beautiful, but dangerous. That's true of a lot of places out west. Our provisions are about gone. We're hungry all the time. They say that if one of us emigrants isn't hungry, then he's sick. I added it up today—we've been on the trail for four days short of six months.

Love, Joseph

ANNIE: November 9, 1850

Dear Grandma,

We're here! We made it! We picked a beautiful place near a fine stream. It's all forest now, of course, but soon it will be our new home. Want to hear something funny? In order to have shelter while we get a crop planted, we bought a wagon from a family who took the overland route. It feels pretty familiar. We're not emigrants anymore!

Love, Annie

From *Read-Aloud Plays: Pioneers*, by Dallas Murphy, Scholastic Professional Books, 1998

WESTWARD BOUND, 1849

The diary entries below were written by Samuel Murray Stover. He left his East Tennessee home in the early months of 1849 with a caravan bound for California, but he did not begin his diary until May 1, when he reached Independence, Missouri.

The published version of his diary was copied from Stover's original diary in 1932 by his granddaughter, Florence Stover Atkins, and great-grand-daughter Almena Atkins.

May 1, 1849—
Encamped half a mile south of Independence, Mo. Associated with the Tennessee Company which is composed of Wm. C. Taylor, Jno. E. brown, Chas. Mason, J.E.T. Harris and myself. We have agreed to each furnish an equal share of the outfit to mine together and to make an equal division of the proceeds of our labor at the end of twelve months after our arrival at the diggins in California.

June 1—
One month is gone and we have traveled two hundred miles. Several sick not able to travel, lay by all day to rest animals and wait on sick. Day fine, some of the company saw a party of Indians. They [are] reported to be Pottawattomies hunting a party of Pawnees who had committed some depredations on their stock.

June 13—
Last night we were visited by one of those prairie storms that I have heard speak of and never would have believed if I had not seen it. The wind blew very hard and the rain came down in perfect torrents. It was with difficulty that we could prevent our tents from being blown over....Struck up the soul-stirring chorus of "Oh California, That's the Land for Me" but lightning began to glare so vividly and the thunder sounded so deep and near that I concluded my song rather quickly....

June 16—
...We saw some 500 buffaloes crossing the river today....

June 24—
...Passed the "Court House Rock" which can be seen some ten miles and is a circular rock standing alone on the plains six miles from the road. It is 400 feet high... Here we are in sight of the Chimney Rock, which looks like the spire of some far off church... Camped this evening at Chimney Rock... This rock...if it can be called a rock[,]...seems to have been formed by the action of the wind and rain on some high hill....

July 15—
Owing to the scarcity of grass in the vicinity we have to drive our mules off some three or four miles... Several hundreds [sic] wagons passed during the day and the creek is again white with wagons and tents and the bottom alive with stock. Made a swing in our wagon for [the sick] Mr. Harris to ride in....

July 24—

…Nooned at a small creek of good water and wood. Filled with fine mountain trout. Camped at a small creek.…Fine grass and water. Sat up tonight to bake bread. Had just laid down to sleep when I was aroused by the clattering of hoofs and the cry of "stampede." Got out as soon as I could and saw the last mule running as fast as he could. Followed them a mile where we came up with them all and took them back.…

⊰✹⊱

August 23—

…moved on two or three miles to better grass and boiling water [hot springs].… Immense crowds of oxen and mules on the grass. The water is so hot it will scald an ox to death in a few moments. Several were laying dead in the springs.… We have now been traveling over a great desert which looks like a bed of ashes and sand.

⊰✹⊱

August 26—

On rising this morning I…learn[ed] that one of our mules had died during the night.… It had shown no signs of disease.… I felt as though I had lost a friend. Such is our attachment to the dumb beasts that have carried us so far.…

August 31—

Today we crossed the Sierra Nevadas. Took us about three hours to cross it… When we came to the top a beautiful forest of tall and stately pines burst upon our vision… Camped in a valley at the base. ten miles. Night cool.…

⊰✹⊱

September 12—

…Camped at a small stream where we found some soldiers with flour, etc. for the troops who were out exploring. Partly intended, I suppose, for the starving immigrants. Thursday, Friday and Saturday completed our journey across the steep and rugged hills and came to the Davis settlement.

THE END

Source: Samuel Murray Stover Collection, Western History Collections, University of Oklahoma Library

MAP OF THE OREGON AND CALIFORNIA TRAILS

After crossing the rocky Mountains, the two trails west parted. The Oregon Trail continued northwest and the California Trail headed due west.

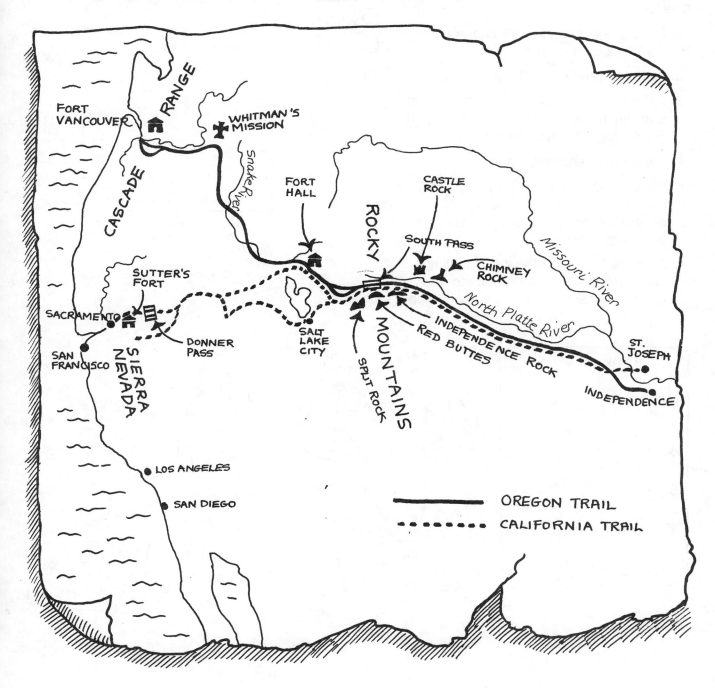

PRAIRIE DOG POP-UP

Materials for 1 Prairie Dog Pop-Up:

4- x 6-inch index card; colored pencils
or crayons; tape (preferably double-sided)

Directions

1. Cut a 1- x 4-inch strip off one end of
   the index card.

2. Color the prairie dog, below.

3. Carefully cut out the prairie dog and tape
   it to the 1- x 4-inch strip. Trim around the
   prairie dog's head and shoulders.

4. Color the prairie dog mound.

5. Cut out the prairie dog mound and tape it to
   an index card. Fold the index card in half and
   cut out the half-moon-shaped opening to the
   prairie dog hole.

6. Tape the bottom of the card, leaving a small
   opening at the top of the mound through
   which to insert the prairie dog and pop it up.

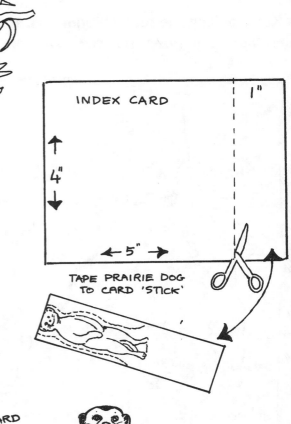

INDEX CARD

1"

4"

← 5" →

TAPE PRAIRIE DOG
TO CARD 'STICK'

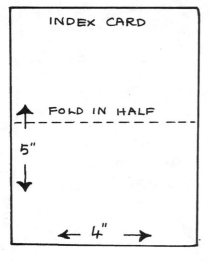

INDEX CARD

FOLD IN HALF

5"

← 4" →

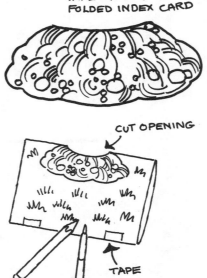

TAPE MOUND TO
FOLDED INDEX CARD

CUT OPENING

TAPE

Part 4

SETTLING THE GREAT PLAINS

1860s–1880s

INTRODUCTION

A wave of settlement on the Great Plains followed the Civil War. People were *pulled* by the free land offered in the Homestead Act of 1862 (160 acres to qualifying pioneers willing to live there for five years) and *pushed* by events limiting opportunities in other parts of the world. In all, about 12 million immigrants from Europe came to the United States between 1865 and 1900, and many of them headed west.

In Part 4, students look at how railroads promoted settlement in the west, inventions contributed to the success of farming the Great Plains, and challenges specific to homesteading shaped the settler culture.

ACTIVITIES

The Great American Desert

Students learn about the characteristics of the Great Plains, an area that pioneers in the 1840s and 1850s, passing through on their way to Oregon and California, considered uninhabitable.

MATERIALS

Map of the United States showing topographic features (mountains, plains)

BACKGROUND

Their maps called it the Great American Desert, and the pioneers headed for Oregon in the 1840s couldn't imagine that anyone would ever choose to settle in this dry, barren area west of the 100° meridian. Technically, the area is not a desert, despite the fact that no trees grow there, because it annually receives 15 to 30 inches of precipitation. But early pioneers viewed it as dry and barren.

However, after the Civil War, lured by the Homestead Act's promise of free land, new waves of pioneers, many of whom were immigrants from Europe, spread across the Great Plains of Kansas, Nebraska, Minnesota, and the Dakotas. The vastness of the land, severity of the weather, and scarcity of settlements exhilarated some homesteaders and intimidated others. Soon the spreading network of railroads had changed the face of the western landscape.

WHAT TO DO

⊛ Ask students to locate the Great Plains on the map, identifying the states that are contiguous.

⊛ Present to students the three key reasons the Great Plains were settled after the Civil War:

1. Railroads made travel to the West easy, fast, and cheap. Railroad companies' advertisements about the benefits of settling on the Plains were published in the eastern United States and in Europe. The ads paid off. In one year, 1882, 105,000 Swedes and Norwegians came to the northern Plains, to what is now the states of Minnesota and North and South Dakota.

2. During the 1870s and early 1880s, the Plains received heavier rainfall than usual. Inventions such as the steel plow and reaper made farming easier. Thus farming was successful, and initial successes attracted more settlers.

3. The Homestead Act of 1862 made land free to settlers.

⊛ Ask students to work in small groups to research and report on one of these three reasons for settlement of the Great Plains. Ask them to answer these questions in their reports:

1. What did the railroad ads say about the Great Plains to attract settlers? What *pushed* so many Scandinavians to emigrate to the United States in the 1870s and 1880s?

2. How did the rainfall affect settlement? How much rain fell in the 1870s and early 1880s? What happened later in the 1880s?

3. What were the requirements of the Homestead Act? What did a settler have to do to qualify for free land? Who was eligible under the Act, and what were the restrictions? Could a nineteen-year-old man file a claim? Could an unmarried woman over age twenty-one file a claim under the Act?

⊛ After the research is completed, discuss the following questions in small groups: What did people need to bring with them to settle on the Great Plains? How did their needs differ from those of the settlers in Oregon in the 1840s? (*All needed food, water, and*

52

shelter; in Oregon there were trees and water for building and irrigating land; on the Great Plains there were no trees to use for building, and the prairie sod had to be broken up before it could be planted.)

EXTEND THE LESSON

Pose the following question to students: In the next 25 years, if settlement of Mars became possible, and land was offered to people willing to settle there, would you consider homesteading on Mars? What would you gain by settling on Mars? What you be giving up? Invite them to write their answers in their journals and then share their entries with the class.

. . . .

From Wagon Trails to Iron Rails

Students interpret the impact of the railroads on western settlement.

MATERIALS

Working on the Railroad; Rich Farming Lands!; U.S. Railroad Map, 1869; Railroad Lifeline reproducibles (pages 60–63); and a map of the U.S. showing topographic features

BACKGROUND

The first Transcontinental Railroad was completed in 1869. Spanning the continent, it spurred on the settlement and economic emergence of the West. The railroad made it possible to ship cattle, corn, and grain to distant markets, and some of those markets grew into large cities, such as Denver, Colorado; Salt Lake City, Utah; and Portland, Oregon. The railroad could make or break a town by adding or eliminating it as a stop. Thus the railroad companies were very powerful.

Railroads also played a powerful role in the eventual subjugation of Native Americans on the Great Plains. Railroads enabled the settlers to rapidly increase their numbers in what was then thought of as Indian territory, putting enormous pressure on those Native Americans

who were still resisting relocation to reservations. By cutting across migratory trails and making it easier for hunters to reach the buffalo herds, railroads speeded up the decimation of the buffalo, on whose existence Native Americans relied.

WHAT TO DO

✸ Distribute copies of the Working on the Railroad and U.S. Railroad Map, 1869 reproducibles to students.

✸ After they have read Working on the Railroad, have them look at U.S. Railroad Map, 1869 and a U.S. topographic map to compare the physical challenges of laying track for the Central Pacific and Union Pacific. Ask: Which railroad would you have preferred working for?

✸ Remind students that the companies that built the transcontinental railroad (Union Pacific and Central Pacific) were given federal land on either side of the tracks they built. Answers to the reproducible questions: 1) 415,200 2) $32,000; $320,000

✸ Reproduce and distribute Rich Farming Lands! Ask students to use a map of the United States to locate the Platte River in Nebraska. Ask: Which railroad circulated this ad? (*Union Pacific*) What "highway" is meant in the following quote from the ad: "…adjoining the world's highway from Ocean to Ocean"? (*the transcontinental railroad*) How does the ad describe the area to be settled? ("…*central belt of population and commerce…*") What does that mean? (*an area where lots of people live and have businesses*)

✸ Distribute the Railroad Lifeline reproducible. Ask: How do the two excerpts on the page differ? (*The first is upbeat and exaggerated; the second is more serious.*) Help students understand that while the railroad sounds like a key to Lancaster's glorious future, Lancaster was also completely dependent on the railroad for supplies.

✸ Ask: Was the coming of the railroad good for all settlers and settlements?

EXTEND THE LESSON

Compare travel by train in the 1870s to travel by covered wagon in the 1840s. Ask students to find out and report on how many miles a train could cover in a day, how comfortable the trains were, and how much the journey cost. Have them compare their findings with what they learned about travel by wagon. Traveling by train means following a schedule. Have students read about the influence train travel had on establishing standardized time in the Close Ups on page 58.

Staking a Claim, Settling In

Students learn about the trying, sometimes deadly conditions faced by homesteaders on the prairie.

MATERIALS

Home Sweet Soddy and What's Happening Here? reproducibles (pages 64–65)

BACKGROUND

In Kansas and Nebraska, 224,500 acres were claimed during the first six months after the passing of the Homestead Act. Many families or groups filed more than one claim. Large land interests (groups of investors) were able to gobble up many claims and were unintended beneficiaries of the Homestead Act.

The earliest homesteaders claimed land that was wooded and near water in eastern Kansas and Nebraska. But later arrivals, whose claims were out on the prairies, had great difficulties farming the tough sod and enduring the Great Plain's natural onslaughts, among which were tornadoes, blizzards, drought, prairie fires, and locusts that devoured crops. And, of course, the immigrants struggled also with an unfamiliar language and culture.

Claims for land were filed through the next two decades; in 1885 alone, 13,301 were filed in Nebraska and 11,874 in Kansas. Many were abandoned. From 1880 to 1889, a total of 41,321,472 acres of land were claimed in the Dakotas.

WHAT TO DO

⊗ Distribute Home Sweet Soddy and make sure students understand that sod refers to the top layer of grass and soil of a field, a lawn, or a prairie. The prairie sod the settlers encountered was very different from commercial sod available today for lawns. Sod sold today is a thin layer of grass, not the thick, tangled mass of long grass and roots that was the prairie's topmost layer.

⊗ Go over the information on the reproducible and discuss the building of sod houses. Ask: What would you like best about living in a soddy? When would you appreciate your soddy more—winter or summer? What would you dislike most about living in a soddy?

⊗ If sod is available, have students cut small pieces to build a model sod house.

⊗ Distribute What's Happening Here? and discuss how the weather and other conditions affected settlers on the Great Plains.

EXTEND THE LESSON

Arrange for a class visit to a sod farm or garden center. Investigate sod, plows, and other farming or gardening tools and, if possible, procedures. Students can read about two special groups of settlers, the Exodusters and Sooners, in the Close Ups on pages 58–59.

Technology Transforms the West

Students learn about inventions that enabled settlers to survive and prosper on the prairie, and they build model windmills.

MATERIALS

Wind Power! reproducible (page 66), 6-ounce paper cups, 4- x 6-inch index cards, plastic coffee can lids, large and small paper clips, 8-inch pieces of string, tape, quarters

BACKGROUND

Reaper, 1834: Cyrus McCormick invented a mechanical reaper, a machine pulled by horses

54

for harvesting grain crops. The reaper made it possible for farmers to grow wheat and other grains in quantities much larger than those needed for their survival because it let them harvest crops four times faster than by hand. Faster harvests led to more planting, and wheat production in the Midwest soared. After 1848 the McCormick Harvesting Machine Company mass-produced reapers and became the nation's largest manufacturer of farm equipment. By 1860, 100,000 had been sold.

Steel Plow, Late 1830s: John Deere invented the steel-bladed plow, which could cut through the sod and made it possible to successfully farm the prairie. By 1857, Great Plains farmers were buying 10,000 plows a year.

Windmill, 1854: Finding water was essential for settlers on the Great Plains; without water on a claim, the prospects were poor. Once a well had been dug, water had to be raised to the surface. In 1854 Daniel Halladay invented a windmill that could be used to turn a shaft that would draw water up from deep wells. The continuous prairie winds provided the energy for the windmills, which could be ordered from mail-order catalogs. Plans were sold so that farmers could also build their own windmills. By the 1880s thousands of windmills were turning on farms on the Great Plains, bringing up water to be used for livestock, irrigation, and human needs.

WHAT TO DO

⊗ Distribute the Wind Power! reproducible and have pairs of students make simple windmills that pull up paper clips. Make sure students understand that full-size windmills do not pull up buckets of water but rather turn a shaft fastened to a pump that draws up the water.

EXTEND THE LESSON

Assign a group of students to report on the process of turning grain into flour, which is then made into bread. Illustrate the report with samples of whole grains (transport them in resealable plastic bags) and whole grain bread. Also, invite a student's bread-making family

member to demonstrate bread making to the class. (If no oven is available, have a demonstration of mixing, kneading, and setting dough to rise, followed by a snack of a previously baked homemade loaf.)

Invite students to read about the impact of barbed wire in the Close Ups section on page 59.

· ·

Life on the Prairie

Students learn about the pioneer way of life on the Great Plains—how they coped with the weather, animals, and isolation, and how they amused themselves.

MATERIALS

What's Happening Here? (page 65) and Pioneer How-To's reproducible (page 67)

Paper Quilts

squares of cardboard or oaktag, 5-inches or longer; colored paper; patterned wrapping or wallpaper; white paper; markers; crayons; scissors; glue stick; tape

Musical Instruments

15-ounce (or larger) cylindrical containers (like oatmeal boxes), string, pencils, scissors

BACKGROUND

Life on the prairie was lonely and hard; pioneers had to work wild, resistant land almost every day in weather that ranged from blazing hot and dry to ferocious with rain, hail, or snow storms. The farming technology discussed in the previous activity may have given farmers the illusion of control, but weather, pests, and prairie fires were both unpredictable and uncontrollable.

Since their land holdings were so large, in order to socialize, pioneers traveled miles, and visits could last a long time, especially if a prairie storm hit. Most of the time, though, the pioneer spirit of "make-do" defeated loneliness. Homemade fun—making something out of nothing—was an important aspect of pioneer life on the prairie.

WHAT TO DO

⊛ Distribute What's Happening Here? and read it aloud or let students do so. Then assign small groups of students to discuss, investigate further, and report on either the Great Plains plague of locusts in the 1870s, the blizzard of 1888, or the Kansas drought of 1860–1861. In their reports, students should identify the problem the pioneers confronted and explain its effect. In conclusion, students decide if they would have gone back east or stuck it out.

⊛ Distribute Pioneer How-To's and read the first quotation aloud, defining unfamiliar words, and then discuss the attitude it conveys. (Consider making it your classroom motto!)

⊛ Talk about why making quilts from old clothes and homemade musical instruments demonstrates the spirit of the opening quotation. Invite students' family members who are quilters, instrument builders, or musicians to visit the class to demonstrate their craft or art.

Explain that many pioneers carried treasured musical instruments with them on their journey west (remember Pa's fiddle in the *Little House* books by Laura Ingalls Wilder). Others made instruments from whatever was at hand, such as dried gourds (rattles), blocks of wood (clappers and drums), or sticks and string (bass fiddles).

Patchwork quilts were made of pieces of fabric, often from old clothes, carefully cut and *patched* together and sewed onto cotton batting to make warm coverings. A "quilting bee" was a social event. When possible, women gathered to help one another arrange and sew individual quilt squares to the backing.

⊛ Have students make either a musical instrument or a paper quilt, following the directions on the reproducible.

⊛ Completed quilt squares can be arranged and displayed on a bulletin board. Individual quilt squares make great note cards or invitations; students can write their messages on the backs.

⊛ Ask one or more volunteers to research and report on some of the quilt patterns used by pioneers.

EXTEND THE LESSON

First, have students create a Weather Tracker chart with the headings: Date, Area of Great Plains, Precipitation, and Temperature.

Now have individual or groups of students track the weather in one area of the Great Plains for 30 days. Students can use on-line reports from the National Weather Service (http://www.nws. noaa.gov/), the Weather Channel (http://www. weather.com), a daily newspaper that gives national weather statistics, or national weather reports on radio or TV.

Students can make periodic journal entries in which they comment on the weather today as if they were homesteaders in the 1870s.

. . . .

School on the Range

Students learn what school was like for pioneer children.

MATERIALS

School Days reproducible (page 68)

BACKGROUND

Schools in pioneer communities were only in session when farm work allowed. With a shortage of trained teachers, many teenage students became teachers themselves. Sometimes a prospective teacher only had to demonstrate an ability to read to be hired. Teachers in isolated, one-room schools lived with their pupils' families, often moving from one home to another. Discipline was a problem, and some teachers used whips and sticks to control their pupils. Most children welcomed the social aspect of school and the break from their daily round of chores. Without books or other materials, pupils had to memorize and then recite lessons in grammar, math, and geography. Schools were the focus of social events in the community, and families would gather there for spelling bees, recitations, and other events.

WHAT TO DO

⊛ Turn your classroom into a one-room schoolhouse for a day. Distribute the School Days reproducible and go over it with students. Then hold a spelling bee in which two teams compete for prizes (maybe classroom privileges); read excerpts from an 1880s school book; memorize and recite math facts; and play old-fashioned games, such as tag, hide-and-seek, and tug-of-war.

⊛ Have students write about the experience in their journals.

⊛ Have students make a list of all the things they would have to give up to recreate the experience of an evening in a frontier town, such as electricity, gas cooking, running water, indoor bathrooms, heating in each room, air conditioning, malls, and cars. Ask volunteers to spend a week without TV or computer games and instead to read, play nonelectric games, and talk with their families and friends.

⊛ To extend this exercise, have students' volunteer to go through an evening without electricity or other modern inventions and write about the experience in their journals.

EXTEND THE LESSON

Conduct a Pioneer Day, or even Week, during which students dress like pioneers and spend some of the day studying what pioneer children would have studied. Or they can present reports on aspects of life for homesteaders on the Great Plains and on individual homesteaders, both famous and unknown, in order to bring the pioneer experience to life. End the day or week with a Great Plains Festival at which authentic pioneer food, such as lemonade and home-baked bread can be served (ask volunteers to prepare the dishes).

CLOSE UPS

The Exodusters—Freedom-Seeking Pioneers

When government troops left the South in 1877, it signaled the end of the period of Reconstruction after the Civil War. Many African Americans also left the South at that time, escaping the threat of continued violence and oppressive, racist laws.

Some African Americans headed west to pursue the American dream of owning land and finding new economic opportunities. During the Great Exodus, which took place from 1875–1879, 50,000 African Americans left the south. They were called Exodusters, after the biblical Exodus, because they believed they were heading to their promised land. Although many moved to Kansas, some went to Oklahoma and on to other points west.

The migration was difficult. There was little chance for organization or planning, and many African Americans did not have the resources to make the journey. Many walked hundreds of miles, facing violence and hostility along the way. Despite these obstacles, many African-American migrants settled in the West during this time.

On Time

In 1882, representatives of all railroad companies in the United States met to establish a standard time. Until then local areas set their own times, based on the position of the sun. Within the same state, there could be dozens of different local times. The spread of railroads had created a need for a standardized time.

The solution, which went into effect in 1883, was to create four time zones: Eastern, Central, Mountain, and Pacific. Within each time zone all clocks were set to the same time, even though that meant "noon" in some places did not correspond to the position of the sun.

The new time-zone boundaries were based on the distance the sun appears to travel in an hour—about 15° of longitude, or 1,000 miles. (Lines of longitude are imaginary north–south lines circling the earth that, along with imaginary east–west lines of latitude, enable navigators to pinpoint their location on the earth's surface.)

CLOSE UPS

Cattle Empires and Barbed Wire

Cattle ranchers prospered on the prairies after the coming of the railroads made it possible to raise cattle in the West and sell it in markets back East. Cowboys were hired to herd the cattle, round them up, and drive the herds to the trains.

Farmers on the Great Plains resented having thousands of cattle cross their land and trample their crops. The invention of barbed wire in 1874 gave farmers a way to fence their land cheaply and effectively. Restricting where cattle could go protected crops but caused conflict with cattle ranchers.

Increasing numbers of settlers and their barbed wire fences, the spread of railroads, and the stormy winter of 1886–1887, during which thousands of cattle died, spelled the end of free-ranging cattle and long-distance cattle drives. Western ranchers turned to barbed wire to confine their herds, which resulted in healthier, more profitable cattle.

The Sooners—Land-Grabbing Pioneers

Two million acres of fertile land in Oklahoma was coveted by eager homesteaders, who considered it public land and theirs by right. However, the land was originally and by law a homeland to 55 Native American tribes, granted to them by the United States government. After being swayed by the homesteaders' arguments, Congress decided to purchase the two million acres of this uninhabited land from the Native Americans and organized a land "run," during which plots could be claimed by white settlers. The land run was held on April 22, 1889. On this day, over 100,000 homesteaders, called Boomers, were told to surround the land and wait for a signal at noon. When they heard the signal, they could race on foot (or by horse, bicycle, or slow-moving train) to claim plots of land.

Some of the homesteaders (later called Sooners) cheated. Instead of waiting until noon, they slipped through the army lines the night before and hid behind bushes and in trees. Their head start enabled them to claim many of the best plots. Because the Sooners obtained land unfairly, the government confiscated the plots of those it could prove had cheated.

By the evening of April 22, 1889, the two million coveted acres were claimed. Overnight, new towns sprung up. Later these towns became cities, such as Guthrie, Oklahoma City, Kingfisher, Stillwater, and Norman. Over the next few years, much of the remaining Indian Territory was purchased by the government and settled by pioneers in additional land runs. The Native Americans were pushed onto less desirable land set aside for reservations.

WORKING ON THE RAILROAD

In 1862, Congress determined the route for the transcontinental railroad. The tracks would follow the pioneer trails along the Platte River, head through the Rockies at South Pass, and continue on across the Great Basin to California. Two railroad companies would build the railroad: the Central Pacific (CP) would start building in the West, moving east; the Union Pacific (UP) would start in the East and move west. Rivalry between the two companies included contests to see who could work faster.

Here's What They Did

THE CENTRAL PACIFIC

Miles of Track Laid: 742 from Sacramento, California, to Promontory Point, Utah

Workers: Mostly Chinese immigrants hired in Hong Kong and Canton and brought to California to work on the railroad

Main Achievement: Blasting 15 tunnels through solid rock in order to lay track across the Sierra Nevada Mountains during blizzards and broiling heat

Human Cost: More than 1,200 Chinese are believed to have died. Many died in blasting accidents and avalanches.

THE UNION PACIFIC

Miles of Track Laid: 1,038 from Omaha, Nebraska, to Promontory Point, Utah

Workers: Irish and other European immigrants, African Americans

Main Achievements: Building the railroad under attack by Sioux and Cheyenne warriors; battling the weather on the Great Plains

Here's What They Got

The U.S. Government gave the railroad companies:

- ⊛ 6,400 acres of federal land on either side of the tracks for every mile completed (later sold to settlers for $2.50 an acre)
- ⊛ $16,000 per mile of level track
- ⊛ $32,000 across the plateaus
- ⊛ $48,000 per mile in the mountains

Do the Math!

1. Use the information below to figure out how many sledgehammer strokes were needed to lay 1,038 miles of track.

     3 strokes to a spike

     10 spikes to a rail

     400 rails to a mile

How many strokes were needed?_____

2. How much money would a railroad company make by selling the acres it acquired for laying one mile of track? How much would it make by selling ten miles worth of land? (See Here's What They Got, above.)

RICH FARMING LANDS!

Railroad companies used posters like this one to attract settlers to the prairie.

U.S. RAILROAD MAP, 1869

The "Last Spike Ceremony" which joined the Union Pacific and Central Pacific railroads took place at Promontory Summit in Utah Territory on May 10, 1869. Find Promontory Summit on the map.

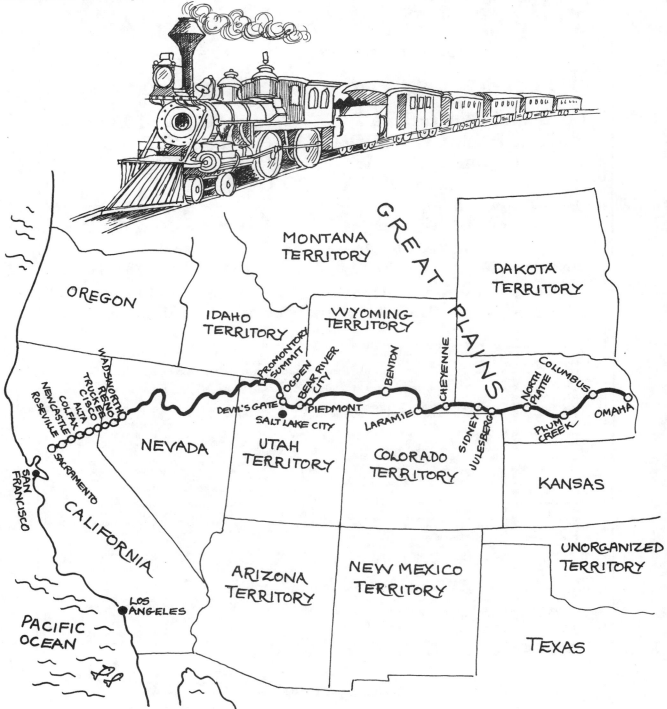

RAILROAD LIFELINE

All Aboard for Lancaster!

Stranger. . .ours is the real thing, up-to-date civilization. Have we done all this in only seven months? Yes, in April the first ten-penny nail was driven home and our first building reached its lofty height to the sky. . . .You really mean to say you've never seen a boom town all set to step out? Stranger, here's the chance of a lifetime. We'll let you in on the ground floor. . .

Glance over the splendor. . . .What about the biggest hotel in the Territory! . . . And talk about court houses, why, ours is painted. Sidewalks? We have 'em to burn, two long ones, even if the streets look like the long ago. . . .See the noble buildings along Railroad Avenue. . . . Minneapolis is getting nervous and Chicago soon will be.

Today, take note that the population of the City of Lancaster stands at exactly 387. . . .And now, Stranger, we come to the real thing. The railroad! . . . Our trains come from the East. . . from Minneapolis and Chicago. Note that the entire world can now reach Lancaster.

And yet there are a few . . .who will say that ours is nothing but a raw prairie town! . . .Hear that? the whistle of a railroad locomotive. Nothing less. And now its bell is clanging. The whistle blows again and again. . . . Do you hear the cheers?

The first train is pulling in to Lancaster!

—from *Dakota in the Morning* by William Harlowe Briggs, © William Harlowe Briggs, Farrar & Rinehart, 1942.

Waiting for the Train

And still the train did not come. . . .

The blizzard winds had blown earth from the fields where the sod was broken, and had mixed it with snow packed so tightly in the railroad cuts that snowplows could not move it. The icy snow could not melt because of the earth mixed with it, and men with picks were digging it out inch by inch. It was slow work because in many. . .[places] they must dig down twenty feet to the steel rails.

April went slowly by. There was no food in the town. Except the little wheat left from the sixty bushels. . .brought in the last week of February. Everyday Ma made a smaller loaf and still the train did not come. . . .

"There's no way to get a team and wagon out to the east," Pa said. "All the roads are under water. . . .If worst comes to worst, a man can walk out on the railroad ties, but it's more than a hundred miles to Brookings [nearest town] and back. . . . They ought to get a train here inside of a week."

"We can make the wheat last that long," Ma said.

—from *The Long Winter* by Laura Ingalls Wilder, © Laura Ingalls Wilder, 1971, HarperCollins, 1971.

HOME SWEET SODDY

Sod House Facts

1 16- x 20-foot house	=	1 acre of sod
1 acre of sod	=	about 90 tons

How Do You Build a House Where There Are No Trees?

Early settlers on the Great Plains cut sod, the thick, root-choked earth beneath their feet, into blocks 1 foot long, 2 feet wide, and 4 inches thick. Each block weighed about 50 pounds. Then they stacked the blocks like bricks to make the walls of a house, called a soddy. The floor was dirt. The roof was made of panels of sod, grass-side up, laid over branches and brush. Sometimes the soddy was built into a hill. Then a cow might be kept on the roof.

Sod House Pros & Cons

Pros

⊗ Naturally more insulated (cooler in summer, warmer in winter) than wooden houses

⊗ Safer from tornadoes and fires than wooden houses

⊗ Cheap (sod was free)

Cons

⊗ Attractive to snakes and mice

⊗ Inhabited by fleas and other insects

⊗ Leaky and muddy in rain (even after the sun came out)

⊗ Dusty when dry from dirt sifting through roof and wall cracks

WHAT'S HAPPENING HERE?

Blizzard

The "Schoolchildren's Blizzard" struck in January 1888. O.W. Coursey was a schoolboy in Dakota Territory that year. He recalled its arrival:

"At recess. . .we were out playing in our shirt sleeves, without hats or mittens. Suddenly we looked up and saw something coming rolling toward us with great fury from the northwest, and making a loud noise. It looked like a long string of bales of cotton. . . each about twenty-five feet high; above them it was perfectly clear."

Like other children, Coursey spent the night in the school. In some parts of the prairie the teachers and students burned desks to keep warm. In another part of the Dakotas, children left the school and were caught by the storm within six feet of a nearby house. They spent the night in a pile of straw; the storm was so heavy they had no idea how close to safety they were.

— *The Pioneers,* Time-Life Books

⊰❀⊱

Drought

When the wind starts blowing I have to go out and hold down every grain of my land. My whole place dried up and blew away.

—Meridel Le Sueur, *North Star Country* (American Folkways series, edited by Erskine Caldwell), Duell, Sloan & Pearce, New York, 1945.

⊰❀⊱

Grasshoppers

Kansas, August 1, 1874

"They began toward night, dropping to earth, and it seemed as if we were in a big snowstorm. . . . Alighting to a depth of four inches or more, the grasshoppers covered every inch of ground, every plant and shrub. Tree limbs snapped under their weight. . ..Quickly and cleanly, these. . .pests devoured everything in their paths. No living plant could escape. Whole fields of wheat, corn, and vegetables disappeared."

Mary Lyon

—Joanna Stratton, *Pioneer Women*, Simon & Schuster, 1981.

WIND POWER!

Show how the wind works! Make a model windmill.

You'll need:

- ☻ 1 6-oz. paper cup
- ☻ 1 4- x 6-inch index card
- ☻ 1 plastic coffee can lid
- ☻ 1 large and 1 small paper clip
- ☻ 1 8-inch piece of string
- ☻ tape
- ☻ 1 quarter

1. Draw a 3 1/2-inch-diameter circle on an index card by tracing the coffee can lid. Draw lines dividing it into four sections. Place a quarter in the center where the four lines meet and trace around it.

2. Cut along the four lines up to the edge of the center circle. Bend each section in the same direction.

3. Completely unbend the large paper clip and hook it slightly at one end. Tape the hooked end to the center of the circle.

4. Then thread the long end through the sides of the paper cup. Attach the small paper clip to one end of the string. Tie the other end of the string to the end of the straight paper clip.

5. Blow on the pinwheel to raise the small paper clip.

Now you're using wind power!

PIONEER HOW-TO'S

"We got the know-how, and the derring-do, the get-up and the go, the got-to, will-do, must-do and the can-do! Let 'er go!"

—Pioneer Saying

How to Make a Quilt Square

1. Cut geometric shapes (triangle, square, rectangle) from colored, patterned, or white paper. On a square piece of cardboard or oaktag (five inches or larger), arrange the pieces in a pattern or design of your choosing. See the examples below.

2. Glue or tape the pieces to the larger square. You can use a black marker to draw "stitches" around the edges. Sign your name in the lower right-hand corner.

3. Combine your squares with others to make a bulletin-board quilt. You can also use a quilt square as a note or invitation, using the back for your message.

How to Make a Stringed Instrument

1. To make a modern version of a homemade bass fiddle, you'll need a clean, empty cylinder-shaped container (like an oatmeal box); heavy string; scissors; and a pencil.

2. Use the sharp pencil to make a hole in the bottom of the container.

3. Turn the container upside-down and run one end of the string through the hole from the outside. Tie a knot in the string inside the container to anchor it. Then place the container on the floor, open end down.

4. Put your foot on the container to keep it down and pull up on the string until it reaches your waist.

5. Tie the pencil to the string and hold it in one hand while you pluck the string with a finger of the other hand. Lengthen and shorten (and loosen and tighten) the string to make different sounds.

⊗ What happens when you use strings of different lengths and containers of different sizes?

SCHOOL DAYS

What was school like 100 years ago? The chart below compares schools today with schools long ago.

SCHOOL DAYS COMPARED	
Your School	**Frontier School**
water fountain	bucket
restrooms	outhouse
cafeteria	lunch pail
a teacher for each grade	one teacher for all grades
teachers certified by the state	teacher passed a local exam
teachers receive paychecks	teachers could be "paid" in produce
notebooks	students write on slates
students travel on a school bus	students walk to school
students have homework	students work at home (chores)

McGuffey's Primers were popluar school books.

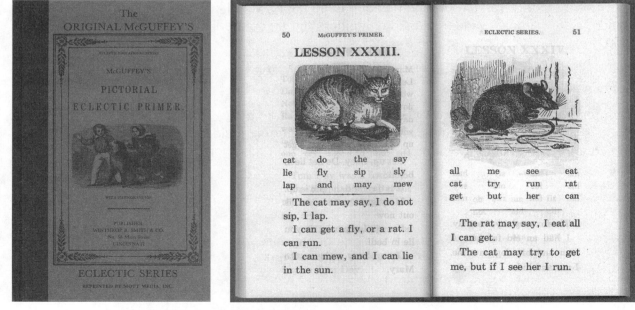

McGuffey's Readers: Facts

    First published: 1836; six editions in all

    Popular for: 75 years

    Total sales: More than 120 million

    No. of states using: 37

    Most sales: In Midwest

Still in print, using 1879 copper plates.

NATIVE AMERICANS: END OF AN ERA

INTRODUCTION

The opening of the West to white settlers changed the way of life of Native Americans forever. By the time the nineteenth century ended, Native Americans had been confined to reservations by the federal government. The buffalo, once the livelihood of Native Americans on the Great Plains, were nearly gone, killed off for their hides and for pleasure by white hunters, many of whom traveled to the plains by railroad just for that purpose. The railroads themselves contributed to the end of the great buffalo herds: The expanding network of tracks disrupted the buffalo's migration.

In this section, students explore the impact westward expansion had on the West's original inhabitants.

Native Americans: Then and Now

Students learn some of the ways western settlement affected Native Americans.

MATERIALS

Indian Lands Maps reproducible (pages 71), library and Internet resources

BACKGROUND

Indian resistance to white settlement of the West began in the 1850s and continued until the late 1880s in response to mounting pressure from the whites to open up more and more Indian Territory to settlement. As Native Americans were pushed onto crowded reservations, they became dependent for food on the often corrupt white Indian agents. Lack of food supplies led to several violent uprisings.

The reservations themselves were relocated and reduced in size to accommodate demands of white settlers. The discovery of gold in the Black Hills of Dakota Territory in 1874 led to violent clashes between prospectors and Indians who were not yet confined to reservations and who held the Black Hills to be sacred. The U.S. Army, which met defeat at the Battle of Little Big Horn under General George Armstrong Custer, pursued the Indians relentlessly and eventually succeeded in killing or bringing most of them onto reservations by 1890.

The last violent encounter was at Wounded Knee Creek in December 1890 when a force of 500 U.S. soldiers surrounded 350 starving Miniconjou Sioux men, women, and children. The Indians were on route to a reservation, and the soldiers began collecting their weapons. When a gun accidentally discharged, soldiers fired into the Sioux encampment with powerful guns. In the end, 250 Sioux were killed. The Wounded Knee massacre, the last "battle" in the Indian Wars, is an enduring reminder of the brutal treatment of Native Americans by whites in the West.

WHAT TO DO

⊗ Read students the following quotation from Senator Eugene Casserly in 1871: "I know what the misfortune of the tribes is. Their misfortune is not…that they are a dwindling race; not that they are a weak race. Their misfortune is that they hold great bodies of rich lands."

⊗ Distribute the Indian Lands Maps to the class and go over the extent of Native American territories in different years. Ask a group of students to identify some of the "rich lands" that Native Americans held at the beginning of the nineteenth century.

⊗ Ask volunteers to read aloud the statements of the Indian leaders. Assign groups of students to prepare brief biographies of the leaders quoted as well as of Geronimo, Crazy Horse, Sitting Bull, and Red Cloud. The reports should include the leaders' birth and death dates (if known), their tribal identification, and discussion of why they are remembered today.

EXTEND THE LESSON

Assign groups of students Native American tribes to investigate and report on. Students should inquire into the traditional life of tribes from the Great Plains, the Northwest, California, and the Southwest. In their reports, groups should describe how the tribes were affected by settlement of the West and how they live today.

INDIAN LANDS MAPS

The three maps below show the extent of Indian lands at different points in our history.

Before Europeons Arrived   **1850**   **1875**

INDIAN LEADERS SPEAK

Ten Bears, Comanche chief, 1867

You said that you wanted to put us on a reservation, to build us houses....I do not want them. I was born upon the prairie, where the wind blew free and there...were no enclosures and everything drew a free breath. I want to die there and not within walls....The white man has the country we loved, and we wish only to wander on the prairie until we die.

    —Ten Bears' speech, Medicine Lodge Creek Treaty Meeting, October 20, 1867.

Chief Joseph, Nez Perce, speech surrendering to General Howard, U.S. Army, 1877

I am tired of fighting. Our chiefs are killed. The old men are all dead....It is cold and we have no blankets. The little children are freezing to death. My people, some of them have run away to the hills, and have no blankets, no food....I want to have time to look for my children, and see how many of them I can find....I am tired. My heart is sick and sad. From where the sun now stands I will fight no more forever.

    —45th U.S. Congress, House of Representatives, 2nd. session.

Black Elk, Oglala [remembering the 1890 massacre at Wounded Knee, at which he was present]

I did not know then how much was ended. When I look back now from this high hill of my old age, I can still see the butchered women and children lying heaped and scattered all along the crooked gulch as plain as when I saw them with eyes still young. And I can see that something else died there in the bloody mud, and was buried in the blizzard. A people's dream died there. It was a beautiful dream....

Chief Joseph, Nez Perce

Whenever the white man treats the Indian as they treat each other, then we will have no more wars. We shall all be alike—brothers of one father, and one mother, with one sky above us and one country around us, and one government for all.

RESOURCES

WEB SITES

African-American History
Exodusters:
www.pbs.org/weta/thewest/wpages/
wpgs100/w171_001.htm
Western Migration and Homesteading:
www.loc.gov/exhibits/african/west.html
General information
http://www.americanwest.com
Information about the route taken by Lewis and Clark
http://www. nps.gov/lecl/
Views of the Missouri River now and at the time of Lewis and Clark
http://www.amrivers.org/l~c.html

CD-ROMS
The Oregon Trail I, 1990; *The Oregon Trail II*, 1994; *Writing Along the Oregon Trail*. MECC, Minneapolis MN, 1-800-685-MECC.

BOOKS
Suitable for elementary grades and up

Brink, Carol Ryrie. *Caddie Woodlawn*. New York: Simon & Schuster (Aladdin paperbacks), 1997.

Capps, Benjamin and the Editors of Time-Life Books. *The Indians*. New York: Time Inc., 1973.

Collins, Carolyn Storm and Christina Wyss Eriksson. *My Little House Crafts Book*. New York: HarperCollins, 1998.

Duncan, Dayton. *The West: An Illustrated History for Children*. Boston: Little, Brown, 1996.

Fisher, Leonard Everett. *The Oregon Trail*. New York: Holiday House, 1990.

Freedman, Russell. *Children of the Wild West*. New York: Scholastic, 1993.

Goble, Paul. *The Return of the Buffaloes*. Washington: National Geographic Society, 1996.

Greenwood, Barbara. *A Pioneer Sampler*. New York: Ticknor & Fields Books for Young Readers, 1995.

Hatch, Lynda. *Pathways of America: The Oregon Trail*. Illinois: Good Apple, 1994.

Hazen-Hammond, Susan. *Timelines of Native American History*. New York: The Berkley Publishing Group, 1997.

Horn, Huston and the Editors of Time-Life Books. *The Pioneers*. Alexandria, VA: Time-Life Books, 1979.

Josephy, Alvin. *500 Nations, An Illustrated History of North American Indians*. New York: Alfred A. Knopf, 1994.

Katz, William Loren. *The Black West*. Seattle: Open Hand Publishing, 1987.

Lawless, Chuck. *The Old West Sourcebook: A Traveler's Guide*. New York: Crown Trade Paperbacks, 1994.

Levine, Ellen. *If You Traveled West in a Covered Wagon*. New York: Scholastic, 1992.

McGovern, Ann. *If You Lived with the Sioux Indians*. New York: Scholastic, 1972.

Murdoch, David. *Eyewitness Books: North American Indian*. New York: Alfred A, Knopf, 1995.

Murphy, Dallas. *Read-Aloud Plays: Pioneers*. New York: Scholastic, 1998.

Peters, Arthur King. *Seven Trails West*. New York: Abbeville Press, 1996.

Ravage, John W. *Black Pioneers: Images of the Black Experience on the North American Frontier*. University of Utah Press, 1997.

Sandler, Martin W. *Pioneers: A Library of Congress Book*. New York: HarperCollins, 1994.

Schlissel, Lillian. *Black Frontiers: A History of African American Heroes in the Old West*. New York: Simon and Schuster, 1995.

_____. *Women's Diaries of the Westward Journey*. New York: Schocken Books, 1992.

Steedman, Scott. *A Frontier Fort on the Oregon Trail*. New York: Peter Bedrick Books, 1993.

Stratton, Joanna. *Pioneer Women: Voices from the Kansas Frontier*. New York: Simon & Schuster, 1981.

Walker, Barbara M. *The Little House Cookbook*. New York: HarperCollins, 1979.

Wilder, Laura Ingalls. *The Little House in the Big Woods; The Little House on the Prairie; On the Banks of Plum Creek; By the Shores of Silver Lake; The Long Winter; The Little Town on the Prairie; These Happy Golden Years*. New York: HarperCollins.

MUSEUMS
Eastern Oregon Museum on the Old Oregon Trail
Haines, OR 97833
(916) 578-3841

Homestead National Monument
Beatrice, NE
(402) 233-3514

Laura Ingalls Wilder Home-Museum
Rt. 1
Box 24
Mansfield, MO 65704

Little House on the Prairie
Box 110
Independence, KS 67301
(316) 331-1890

Oregon Trail Museum/ Scotts Bluff National Monument
Gering, NE 69341
(308) 436-4340

Pioneer Heritage Center
Cavalier, ND 58220
(701) 265-4561

Santa Fe Trail Center/ Ft. Larned National Historic Site
Larned, KS 67550
(316) 285-6911

ORGANIZATIONS
National Frontier Trails Center
P.O. Box 1019
Independence, MO 64051-0519
(816) 254-0059

Oregon Trail Wagon Train
Bridgeport, NE
(402) 586-1850

Oregon-California Trail Association
P.O. Box 1019,
Independence, MO 64051-0519
(816) 252-2276

Laura Ingalls Wilder Memorial Society
Box 269
Pepin, WI 54759